Miranda Threlfall-Holmes is chaplain  College, Durham and Interim Princip
After a degree in history at Cambridge sl ment, then studied for a doctorate in medic. al history at Durham University, lectured part-time at Newcastle University and was a lay volunteer chaplain at the Royal Victoria Infirmary in Newcastle. She trained for ordination at Cranmer Hall in Durham and was a curate at a parish in Heaton. She has been involved in ordination and lay theological training in Durham and Newcastle dioceses for several years: teaching essay-writing skills to adult returners to education, tutoring Church history to trainee readers and ordained local ministers, and being a placement supervisor to ordinands exploring university chaplaincy. As a historian and a theologian she has written and published extensively in both the academic and popular media. Her doctoral thesis, *Monks and Markets: Durham Cathedral Priory 1460–1520*, was published by Oxford University Press in 2005 and she has contributed to the *Church Times*, *The Guardian* and Reuters.

Mark Newitt is a hospital chaplain in Sheffield. Since his first degree in pharmaceutical management he has maintained an interest in health-care, ethics and spirituality. He is particularly interested in the work of chaplaincy within neonatal and maternity units and is currently studying for a doctorate in theology and ministry through Durham University, investigating the benefit of chaplaincy support to bereaved parents following the death of a baby. A member of the Society for the Study of Christian Ethics, he trained for ordination at Cranmer Hall in Durham and was a curate in Northampton before taking up his current post. As well as having a collection of liturgy published in Proost's pocket booklets series, he has had articles on his work published in the *British Medical Journal*, *Practical Theology* and the *Scottish Journal of Healthcare Chaplaincy*.

SPCK Library of Ministry

Being a Chaplain
Miranda Threlfall-Holmes and Mark Newitt

Community and Ministry: An introduction to community
development in a Christian context
Paul Ballard and Lesley Husselbee

Finding Your Leadership Style: A guide for ministers
Keith Lamdin

How to Make Great Appointments in the Church:
Calling, Competence and Chemistry
Claire Pedrick and Su Blanch

Pioneer Ministry and Fresh Expressions of Church
Angela Shier-Jones

Reader Ministry Explored
Cathy Rowling and Paula Gooder

Reflective Caring: Imaginative listening to
pastoral experience
Bob Whorton

Skills for Collaborative Ministry
Sally Nash, Jo Pimlott and Paul Nash

Supporting Dying Children and Their Families:
A handbook for Christian ministry
Paul Nash

Supporting New Ministers in the Local Church:
A handbook
Keith Lamdin and David Tilley

Tools for Reflective Ministry
Sally Nash and Paul Nash

Youth Ministry: A multi-faceted approach
Sally Nash

BEING A CHAPLAIN

SPCK Library of Ministry

Edited by
MIRANDA THRELFALL-HOLMES
and
MARK NEWITT

First published in Great Britain in 2011

Society for Promoting Christian Knowledge
36 Causton Street
London SW1P 4ST
www.spckpublishing.co.uk

The author and publisher have made every effort to ensure that the external website and
email addresses included in this book are correct and up to date at the time of going
to press. The author and publisher are not responsible for the content, quality or
continuing accessibility of the sites.

British Library Cataloguing-in-Publication Data
A catalogue record for this book is available from the British Library

ISBN 978–0–281–06385–7

Typeset by Graphicraft Ltd, Hong Kong
First printed in Great Britain by MPG Books Group
Subsequently digitally printed in Great Britain

Produced on paper from sustainable forests

Contents

Part 3
CHAPLAINS' STORIES – HEALTHCARE

Part 4
CHAPLAINS' STORIES – THE PRISON SERVICE

Part 5
CHAPLAINS' STORIES – OTHER SECTORS

Part 6
THEOLOGICAL REFLECTIONS

Contributors

Joan Ashton (full-time, Anglican priest) worked for 14 years in local government housing management before being ordained in 1993. She has been employed in acute sector healthcare chaplaincy for 12 years, the past 6 as coordinator of chaplaincy services for the Rotherham NHS Foundation Trust and the Rotherham Hospice. She has recently completed a degree in supportive and palliative care at Sheffield Hallam University, in which she focused on the provision of spiritual care within this field of healthcare.

Michael Banfield (full-time, Baptist minister) is senior chaplain at London Luton Airport and senior vice-president, International Association of Civil Aviation Chaplains – <www.iacac.ws>. He is supported equally by the airport operating company and the churches ecumenically through Workplace Ministry – <www.workplaceministry.org.uk>.

Lance Blake (full-time, lay Anglican) has been chaplain at the Rowans Hospice in Portsmouth for the last 11 years. His spiritual journey has centred around the healing ministry in one form or another for the past 40 years, during which time he joined the Franciscan Order. He was instrumental in preparation of the 'Standards for Hospice and Palliative Care Chaplaincy' for the Association of Hospice and Palliative Care Chaplains and worked with the College of Healthcare Chaplains to help form the UK Board of Healthcare Chaplains. He holds a masters degree in chaplaincy and spiritual direction.

John Boyers (part-time, Baptist minister) is the founder and international director of Sports Chaplains Offering Resources and Encouragement (SCORE), a UK-based charity that works interdenominationally to bring quality chaplaincy to the world of sport – <www.scorechaplaincy.org.uk>. He began his chaplaincy work with Watford FC and is now chaplain to Manchester United FC.

Tim Bryan (full-time, Anglican priest) was ordained in 1997 while still serving in the Metropolitan Police. After specializing in the investigation of child abuse and setting up national public protection systems, he joined the Prison Service as a resettlement chaplain. In 2008 he became the coordinating chaplain at HMP Wandsworth.

Bill Burleigh (part-time, Roman Catholic deacon) was ordained in 2001 while still a full-time senior civil servant in the Department of Health. Having retired early in 2005 he completed a masters degree in theology and ministry at Durham University and added chaplaincy to his portfolio of parish and diocesan work.

Dawn Colley (full-time, Methodist minister) is an ecumenical chaplain at HMP Wakefield, a high-security men's prison. Previously she served as a minister in the Leeds Circuit and as a Free Church chaplain at HMP Newhall. Theologically she trained at Durham University, where she has recently completed doctoral research exploring the role of the chaplain with regard to self-harm among female prisoners.

Jim Craig (full-time, Anglican priest) studied fine art at the University of Humberside and the Open University. He trained for ordination at Cranmer Hall in Durham and served his curacy in Stanley in County Durham. Jim was appointed to his current post as community arts chaplain in Bensham and Gateshead in January 2005. He is the only full-time arts chaplain in the Church of England.

Anna de Lange (part-time, lay Anglican) is chaplain to Durham School and a Reader in Durham diocese. She has a background in adminis-tration (having worked as a librarian and a church administrator) and in liturgy (having served for five years on General Synod and the Liturgical Commission of the Church of England). She is a member of the diocesan liturgical committee and of the Group for the Renewal of Worship, and encourages greater participation of lay people in the leadership of worship by leading training events and writing Grove booklets.

Dana Delap (part-time, lay Anglican) was a chaplain at HMP Low Newton and a Reader in Durham diocese until 2009, when she left to train for ordination. She has been a member of General Synod and of the Liturgical Commission for ten years, latterly as vice-chair of the Commission.

Stephen Fagbemi (full-time, Anglican priest) is coordinating and Anglican chaplain at Sunderland University and associate priest at Sunderland Minster. After his theological education and ordination in Nigeria he studied at Nottingham University and later at the University of Kent, Canterbury, where he obtained his doctorate specializing in New Testament and applied theology.

Nigel Goodfellow (full-time, URC minister) was ordained in 1983. He became a chaplain in 1992 and in 2005 the Trust head of chaplaincy, Newcastle upon Tyne Hospitals NHS Trust. An independent assessor for the Human Tissue Authority, his interests lie in medical ethics, critical care, transplantation and paediatrics. He is a visiting lecturer and doctoral student with the Centre for Chaplaincy Studies based at St Michael's College in Llandaff, Cardiff.

Ruth Hake (full-time, Anglican priest) was ordained in 2002. She served her title post at St Michael le Belfrey in York, during which time she was also a Territorial Army chaplain. She joined the RAF as a chaplain in 2005. She is currently force chaplain, British Forces South Atlantic Islands, based in the Falkland Islands.

Chris Hughes (part-time, Roman Catholic priest) is a sessional chaplain to HMPs Acklington and Castington. A priest in the diocese of Hexham and Newcastle, previously he was pastoral director at Ushaw College. He has been chaplain to a mental-health trust, a hospice, a comprehensive school, Newcastle College, Northumbria and Newcastle Universities, L'Arche, the Student Cross Pilgrimage and even a football tournament – Euro 96.

Clare McBeath (full-time job share, Baptist minister) worked for two years as multi-faith chaplain in a large further-education institution in a northern city. She is currently minister of Openshaw Baptist Tabernacle in East Manchester. She has a doctorate in contextual theologies and is a non-executive director of Manchester Mental Health and Social Care NHS Trust. She has been engaged in local regeneration as chair of the Health and Well-Being Programme, as a local school governor and as vice-chair of Brook Manchester. Clare is co-author of *Crumbs of Hope: Prayers from the City* (Peterborough: Inspire, 2006) and of the Dancing Scarecrow worship-resource website – <www.dancingscarecrow.org.uk>.

Ian Maher (full-time, Anglican Church Army evangelist). Since January 2006 he has been the multi-faith chaplaincy coordinator at Sheffield Hallam University. In previous posts he has been head of academic programmes at Wilson Carlile College of Evangelism, Sheffield, where he also taught ethics and world religions; national coordinator of the ecumenical Certificate in Evangelism Studies; and a parish evangelist in south-east London. He has also written extensively about film.

Stephen Robbins (full-time, Anglican priest) trained at King's College London and St Augustine's College, Canterbury, and then worked in parishes in Durham diocese for 11 years before becoming a forces chaplain in 1987. His career since then has been within the forces, including a time as chaplain of the Royal Memorial Chapel, Sandhurst. He is currently Chaplain General Land Forces and Archdeacon for the Army.

Hugh Shilson-Thomas (full-time, Anglican priest) is dean of chapel and chaplain at Selwyn College and chaplain and director of Studies in Theology at Newnham College, Cambridge University. After chaplaincies at Kingston University and Robinson College, Cambridge, and a masters degree at King's College London, he was appointed as the Church of England's national adviser for higher education and chaplaincy, a post he held for five years before leaving to take up his current posts in 2008.

David Simpson (full-time, Anglican priest) was previously Anglican chaplain at the University of Southampton (1997–2005). He joined the Royal Navy in 2005.

Jane Speck (part-time, Anglican priest) is chaplain to King's College London and assistant priest in the North Lambeth parish. She previously worked in parishes in Worcester diocese and is a member of the Iona Community.

Garry Swinton (full-time, Anglican priest) has since 2001 been chaplain in two inner-London church schools: the Grey Coat Hospital, a girls' Church of England comprehensive school, and Westminster City School, a non-denominational church school for boys. He is also priest vicar at St Margaret's Church Westminster Abbey. Before ordination Garry taught religious education in Essex. He has been a parish priest in Surbiton, succentor of Southwark Cathedral, priest in charge of St Faith's Wandsworth and chaplain to Wimbledon YMCA.

Charles Thody (full-time, Anglican priest) is head of chaplaincy for the Rotherham, Doncaster and South Humber Mental Health NHS Foundation Trust. Prior to being appointed to this role he was chaplaincy team manager at Rampton High Security Hospital, where he had a particular interest in dangerous and severe personality disorders.

Andrew Todd is director of the Cardiff Centre for Chaplaincy Studies (Cardiff University and St Michael's College). He has 16 years' experience of theological education and has also been a chaplain in higher education and sub-dean of St Edmundsbury Cathedral. He is a practical theologian with particular interests in chaplaincy, public theology, hermeneutics and research methods. His publications include a number of articles on military chaplaincy.

(Editors' note: the descriptions 'full-time' and 'part-time' used above relate to the contributors' chaplaincy employment only.)

Acknowledgements

The editors gratefully acknowledge the help and support of innumerable colleagues and friends in the conception and writing of this book. First, our thanks must go to our colleagues in our workplaces, Durham University and Sheffield Hospitals, for valuable conversations about what we are doing as chaplains and what our institutions are employing us for, which led to the idea for this book. Particular mention must go to Paula Stirling, Eva Schumacher-Reid, Kate Bruce, Jenny Moberly, Anthony Bash and Jonathan Lawson at Durham; and Mark Cobb, Martin Kerry and Judith Daley at Sheffield. Second, we are extremely grateful to all the chaplains represented here, who willingly gave their time to write up their experiences to share with others. Finally, we gratefully acknowledge the help received from all those who have read and commented on the manuscript, particularly Rob Lawrence and Ken Newitt, who read the whole draft, and from the editorial team at SPCK.

Introduction

MIRANDA THRELFALL-HOLMES
and MARK NEWITT

Introduction

Chaplaincies are a major part of the mission and ministry of Christian churches and are increasingly being valued and entered into by members of other faiths. There remains, however, little common reflection and analysis about what chaplaincy is, what a chaplain might be expected to do and whether and why it is important. This book aims to help chaplains and those considering chaplaincy or ministry more generally to reflect upon these questions and the very varied contexts in which chaplains operate.

Following this initial chapter, which briefly surveys the rapidly changing context in which chaplaincy operates and goes on to discuss the concept of 'marginality', the book is divided into several parts. The first five collect together 22 stories from those engaged in chaplaincy in a variety of contexts. The focus is on the major areas in which chaplains are employed, and takes a deliberately multi-vocal approach. Each broad category of chaplaincy (armed forces, education, healthcare and prisons) is represented by several contributors working in different contexts. There are also contributions from chaplains in airport, sports and arts chaplaincy. While the majority are Anglican, this collection also includes Methodist, Baptist, URC and Roman Catholic contributors. In addition lay and ordained chaplains are represented and several of the contributors work in or coordinate multi-faith teams. This variety illustrates the breadth and diversity of roles that exist within the umbrella title of 'chaplaincy' and also allows common themes to emerge.

Finally, Part 6 consists of four chapters of theological reflections on specific aspects of chaplaincy. For the first, Chapter 23, we invited Andrew Todd to consider multi-faith chaplaincy. He outlines some of the reasons for its development, explores how three areas of public sector chaplaincy have responded and discusses the implications these reactions raise for the future of chaplaincy. In the remaining three chapters of Part 6 the editors, drawing on all that has been before, offer further reflection. Hence Chapter 24 analyses the role(s) that a chaplain fills and the key skills needed by chaplains across the range of institutional contexts in which they minister. Chapter 25 goes on to discuss models of chaplaincy held both by chaplains and also, crucially, by those institutions employing them. Finally, in Chapter 26 issues around institutional values are identified and the tensions delineated in the chaplains' stories are discussed.

The contemporary context

Over the last decade much has changed both in the Church and in the institutions in which chaplains minister. After September 11, the tensions and challenges between secular and faith perspectives are very much on the agenda of public and private institutions. Multi-faith chaplaincy is suddenly in vogue, but conflicting definitions and understandings of it exist. How such understandings are put into practice also varies widely. Meanwhile chaplains in institutions such as prisons and universities are increasingly being seen by government as on the front line of combating religious extremism.

Within the Church many of the tensions between chaplains and parochial clergy identified by Legood (1999) still exist. Indeed, in places they have been exacerbated by lack of funds and clergy 'restructuring' over the decade. In addition other, more subtle changes have occurred to the church context in which chaplaincy operates. For example, increasing numbers of dual-clergy households mean that chaplaincy can be a career choice that enables two ordained clergy each to receive pay for their work (Hancocks et al., 2008).

Against these changing backgrounds, chaplaincies themselves are a major area of ministry for the churches and other faiths. There are around 500 full-time and a further 3,000 part-time chaplains in the NHS in the UK (roughly half of these from the Church of England). Around 320 chaplains are employed in universities in England, Scotland, Wales and Ireland, with perhaps a further 1,000 voluntary associate university chaplains from other faiths and minority denominations. From the Church of England alone there are over 200 ordained chaplains employed by prisons and young-offender institutions. A further 160 are employed by the Army, Navy and Air Force. There are over 170 ordained Church of England chaplains in both private and state schools and many more schools with lay chaplains or a chaplain from another denomination. There are also chaplains at airports, theatres, shopping centres, sports clubs and so on. Through these latter roles many clergy combine part-time or honorary chaplaincy work with church responsibilities.

Ministry on the margins and in the midst

Chaplaincy, often labelled 'sector ministry' as though it only addresses a narrow facet of society, can be seen by the church hierarchy as not just on but beyond the margins of church life proper. A typical view is that 'the core business of the diocese . . . is the ministry of the parishes', as Jackson (2005) declares, while suggesting that a diocese might save money for its 'core business' by cutting chaplaincy funding. Yet from another standpoint the picture looks very different. Chaplains are placed not in churches where people may or may not come looking for them but actually where people are. They are, to use Ballard's (2009) helpful term, 'embedded' in prisons, schools, universities, hospitals, shopping centres, airports, workplaces, battlefields and barracks. There at the time they are wanted, on the spot, many chaplains are on call day and night. Chaplains may be marginal to the churches, but they are often in places where the 90 per cent of the UK population who do not regularly attend church will be found. In marketing terms, chaplains and chaplaincies are gold dust. Like an advertising slot in the middle of a world cup final, they give the Church an opportunity to engage with the unchurched or dechurched majority whom it would otherwise find hard to reach.

In the context of the increased focus on mission and outreach, of fresh expressions and 'mission-shaped' church, it seems perverse that chaplaincy remains so commonly characterized as marginal. In theological reflection on and discussions about chaplaincy, issues of marginality or liminality almost invariably arise. Furthermore, the terms 'marginal' and 'liminal' are often used interchangeably, with various distinct yet overlapping meanings that compound the problem. There are three primary ways in which these terms are used in the context of discussing chaplaincy, some more helpful than others. First, as noted above, the experience of being a chaplain can be one of marginalization. While this may be the case for any minister in our increasingly secular society, it can be doubly so for chaplains who find themselves marginal both to the institution to which they are chaplain and to the church from which they are sent.

Second, the value or distinctive nature of a chaplain's ministry may be perceived as one of liminality – standing between heaven and earth, pointing out the existence of an alternative reality, embodying and being a threshold between the two. Used in this way the term derives from sociology and anthropology, often used of a shaman or similar religious figure. Chaplaincy is not distinct from other ministry in being conceived in terms of liminality. However, the nature of chaplaincy as embedded within a (usually non-religious) organization or institution emphasizes this aspect of the role. The chaplain's very presence opens a doorway between two realms, or at least points to the existence of such a doorway. Images of liminality most obviously lend themselves to contexts such as hospice chaplaincy, the chaplain being seen as the one who helps people to confront and/or cross the threshold between life and

death. It can, though, be extended to other 'thresholds', such as adolescence/
adulthood (education chaplaincy), freedom/imprisonment (prison chaplaincy) and so on.

Third, it can be argued that much chaplaincy occurs in marginal
places. The major employers of chaplains – hospitals, prisons, universities,
schools and the armed forces – are all places that are, to some extent,
marginal to everyday life for those not immediately involved in them.
However important and even central to our society such institutions
may be, they hover on the edges of our consciousness until or unless
they are forced upon our notice. Yet for those within these institutions,
even if only temporarily, they provide an alternative reality. University
students speak of the 'bubble' of university life – even as they travel from
rented houses to lecture theatres, both set in the real world, they feel a
disconnection, speaking of 'real life' as what lies outside the university.
Being in hospital can create a similar experience – patients often feel
that normal family and community life has been disrupted. Likewise
members of the armed forces often struggle to adapt to life in Civvy
Street. In these marginal places, chaplains are amid the very real life that
goes on.

So what kind of ministry goes on in these places? An enormous variety,
as the stories contained in this volume demonstrate. There are, though,
common themes that emerge and that begin to demonstrate that these
'marginal' ministries are in fact very mainstream. Themes that emerge
from the stories that follow include the importance of forging personal
relationships, both in the institutional structures and with the more
transient populations that pass through. The importance of both knowing
people and being known, and of listening attentively and respectfully to
people's stories, is repeatedly stressed in the contributions.

Many of the chaplains writing here speak of their ministry as 'incarnational', emphasizing the theological as well as the practical importance
of presence and relationships. The metaphor of journeying with people
is also a recurring theme. Chaplaincy is above all a ministry of presence,
of simply being there amid things – a sacramental ministry, not primarily
in the 'churchy' sense of celebrating the sacraments but in the theological
one of taking the everyday stuff of life and making it a sign of God's presence and love. It is also an expectant ministry, waiting for opportunities to
present themselves and expecting those opportunities to come.

Chaplains will not often get to follow the lives and careers of those
they interact with at significant moments. We often only see people once
or at most for a few years, and rarely get to see the seeds we have (it is
hoped) planted, watered or tended come to fruition. Accordingly chaplains
have to be extremely good at discernment – at discerning what the
particular task at hand is, getting on with it and then accepting the

next task that comes along. We have to be extremely good at setting boundaries in our own minds and at managing the expectations of others. Finally, we have to learn to live with the tension that comes from serving two masters and often being considered only marginally relevant by both.

Chaplaincy and church ministry

It is clear, therefore, that while chaplaincy has certain distinctive features that differentiate it from parochial ministry, most notably the more transient nature of the relationships that are formed and the population that is served, it is by no means essentially different from church and parish ministry. Furthermore, we would suggest that because chaplains serve in the world of work and are amid society outside of the church structures, their insights and experience are of key importance for the churches – chaplaincy may well be the canary in the mine for the churches' relationship to society. Chaplains seem often to be facing the rapidly arising and changing issues in contemporary society more sharply and more quickly than the rest of the Church (Gilliat-Ray, 1999). Those whose stories are collected together here often describe a sense of alienation from the wider Church arising, at least in part, from the fast-moving and changing contexts in which they operate. Chaplains often have to formulate answers to questions the institutional churches have not yet begun to ask. Andrew Todd, in Chapter 23, discusses the ways in which chaplaincies have responded to the challenges of diversity in faith, individual philosophy and belief, and secular viewpoints. Models of ministry that arise from chaplaincy experience may well be precisely those to which other clergy will need to adapt in years to come.

Any discussion of chaplaincy therefore needs to take place within, and to contribute to, the wider context of the theology and practice of ministry more generally. Chaplains, whether lay or ordained, have a particularly visible and defined representative role within their institutions. They may variously articulate this as representing in themselves either the Church, God or the faith/spiritual dimension in that place. They are representative persons, set aside in some way. Being a chaplain carries with it a representative function and an ontological freight. For this reason, much of what is said about chaplaincy in this book should be read in conversation with the extensive literature on ministry and vocation. In turn, the experiences and reflections of chaplains in a wide variety of contexts that this book provides will shed light on some of the key issues in ministry and ministerial practice facing the wider Church.

It is notable that in much that is written on ministry more generally, 'chaplaincy' is often one of the models presented for this wider ministry.

Sometimes this is a positive model, but often its use is more negative. It has become commonplace to say that parish priests should not be mere chaplains to their congregations. In the context of the recent emphasis in all the mainstream churches upon mission and evangelism, where 'mission-shaped church' has become such a rallying cry, the point being made is that the focus of a minister's work should be not on those who already belong to the church but on those who do not. The term 'chaplain' in this context is used to describe an overly limited role. Those with an evangelical background in particular may be suspicious that chaplaincy leaves no room for mission. Yet all the chaplains represented here speak of their ministry to the whole community in which they are situated. Being a chaplain is precisely the opposite of the overconcentration on the worshipping community that can sometimes be characterized by the term 'chaplaincy'. Mission is a broad category and involves engaging with a community in terms and in ways that are fitting to the particular context. This is at the heart of how most chaplains describe their role.

Given the tensions and fears in the contemporary Church surrounding such issues as faith in public life and the role of the state in pressing forward an equality agenda, the delicate balancing act undertaken by most chaplains provides an important case study in how mission is possible in a secular environment. Billings (2010) has argued that the Church of England requires clergy who are prepared to accept the role of 'chaplain to the nation' and in so doing are prepared to relinquish being too quick to evangelize, too determined to draw boundaries around the membership of the church or acceptable behaviour, and prepared to welcome everyone in and – to some extent at least – give them what they want. This characterization of chaplaincy rings true with the stories told by many of the chaplains in this volume. There is in many quarters of the Church a siege mentality – a sense that the world is becoming a dangerously secular place and that the response of the churches must be to nail their colours to their masts and fight.

Yet the experiences of chaplaincy related here show, gloriously and optimistically, that this is by no means the only possible response. This new, aggressively secular world, in which values such as tolerance, equality, accountability and transparency are consistently expected to trump historic church tradition or belief, has been precisely the context in which chaplains have been operating cheerfully for decades. The 'social contract' implicit in the relationship between the churches and the nation has been explicitly spelt out in contracts, working agreements and policy documents in schools, hospitals, prisons and universities for some time. Chaplains work creatively and productively within these guidelines. The experiences of chaplains can, therefore, be of considerable help in shaping the Church of the future and showing how faith and ministry can flourish in an explicitly secular and even, on occasion, hostile environment.

(In Parts 1–5 the names of people referred to have been changed to preserve anonymity.)

References

Ballard, P. (2009), 'Locating chaplaincy: a theological note'. *Crucible* July/Sep., pp. 18–24.

Billings, A. (2010), *Making God Possible*. London: SPCK.

Gilliat-Ray, S. (1999), 'Sector ministry in a sociological perspective', in Legood, *Chaplaincy*.

Hancocks, G., Sherbourne, J. and Swift, C. (2008), '"Are they refugees?" Why Church of England Clergy enter Healthcare Chaplaincy'. *Practical Theology* 1/2, pp. 163–79.

Jackson, B. (2005), *The Road to Growth: Towards a Thriving Church*. London: Church House Publishing.

Legood, G. (ed.) (1999), *Chaplaincy: The Church's Sector Ministries*. London: Cassell.

Part 1

CHAPLAINS' STORIES –
THE ARMED FORCES

1

The RAF

RUTH HAKE

> They shall grow not old, as we that are left grow old:
> Age shall not weary them, nor the years condemn.
> At the going down of the sun and in the morning
> We will remember them.
>
> (Binyon, 1914)

As I said those familiar words, redolent of childhood Remembrance Sundays spent watching very old men remembering events that occurred many decades before my birth, I suddenly had a moment of resounding clarity. Too often, gathered round some freezing war memorial with those who, it seemed to a child, could never have really been young, I had uttered this poem from the perspective of those grown old. Now, midnight on a freezing runway in the middle of southern Afghanistan, I said those words from the perspective of the young. I was no longer an observer of this rite of remembrance, I was a part of the act. The young man, whose broken body we had carefully placed in his coffin two hours earlier, was being carried aboard the waiting aircraft. He would not grow old.

His repatriation home was also to be my flight home. In the lottery of war, I got to fly home to fill the three years since then with signposts of a life lived – marriage and a baby. For those of us who get to grow old, it is our absolute duty that we never, in our getting old(er), forget those who remain frozen in youth.

Twenty hours after leaving Afghanistan that night, I was at a service station on the M5 motorway in England. As I sat eating my tomato soup, still in desert uniform, with Kandahar sand covering my boots, I was uncomfortably aware of the stares of others. How to explain where I had been? How to readjust to being back in the UK where life continued as normal? How to get anyone here to understand? The sense of unreality pervaded for days if not weeks. I wanted to shout to those around, 'Do you not care what's happening there?' 'Do you have no idea?'

This encapsulates the incarnational nature of forces ministry. It is in living, working, eating, sleeping – and potentially dying – alongside those to whom we seek to minister, that we both earn the right to conduct that ministry and inform and inspire that ministry. Military chaplains can often be looked at askance by our sending churches. We have literally taken the Queen's shilling and could, mistakenly, be seen as 'warmongering' or, at the least, lending countenance to what might be viewed as a morally dubious endeavour. While I believe it would be very difficult to be a military chaplain if one were a thoroughgoing pacifist, it is certainly not true that we are a bunch of militants. No chaplain carries a weapon. Our role is to offer pastoral, moral and spiritual care to those who have regularly risked their lives on behalf of our country, and to the families of those who have lost their lives; to support them as they cope with the inevitable strains and pressures that that brings. Our motivation is the same as any other priest or minister: to serve God and his children and to share the good news of Jesus Christ with those to whom we are sent.

Airmen and women have as many ethical questions about war as anyone else; in fact often rather more as they are faced with the realities of fighting. They also often have philosophical and theological questions that come with being faced with death, although individuals may not recognize that description of their query! In order for chaplains to earn the right to proffer answers, or to educate new recruits on the values and moral dilemmas of RAF life, they have to live the questions alongside those who ask.

As I experienced, there is a disconnection between what is experienced in armed conflict and reintegrating at home. It is very hard to convey the reality to those who have no knowledge of it. For this reason the military turn to chaplains who have shared the experience with them. Obviously there are exceptions to this, and parish clergy may well find themselves ministering to military people. There is, however, an implicit trust in those with whom one serves. An airman or woman has no need to explain a situation to a chaplain; he or she knows that the chaplain already understands. This credibility begins with training. We have to pass the same leadership exercises and fitness tests as any other officer. As we continue, it is done by living in the same, sometimes difficult, conditions and taking the same risks in conflict. As someone in the (currently) unique position of being both RAF chaplain and RAF wife, I can say that it also means living with the same nagging fear of 'the knock at the door' while a loved one is away, and asking our own families to live with that fear as well.

The rewards of this ministry are many. The privilege of being able to offer spiritual and pastoral care to this very special community, through good times and bad, cannot be overestimated. To offer care to the bereaved, ill and injured is part of the core pastoral work of all clergy. However, in our very specific community the situation is often unexpected and sometimes a shocking tragedy. The deceased is often known personally to the chaplain, which can of course hold its own issues, or the chaplain may have a number of families to 'kinform' in the same night. This is clearly where ministry is at its hardest, and it can take its toll on chaplains. Yet it is also where it is vital that we be able to offer Christian hope and the love and care of Christ.

It has been said that in the twenty-first century, parish clergy often deal almost exclusively with those who 'opt in' to their congregations, the old pastoral model of ministry being impossible with huge multi-benefice parishes. The RAF chaplain conversely ministers to a predominantly unchurched community. The practice of 'all souls' ministry means that every single person on a unit or station has the right to expect pastoral care and – importantly – complete confidentiality from the chaplain. What is more interesting, and can be surprising to those not in the military, is that virtually everyone in that community does, at some point, seek that pastoral and spiritual care. The 'Padre', as we are affectionately known, has a uniquely privileged position: able to be a friend and adviser to commanders while offering a confidential listening ear to all service personnel and their families, regardless of rank or belief. 'I'm not religious myself, Padre, but ...' is a common refrain. The ensuing question or comment keeps us on our toes theologically. Engaging with those questioning individuals is exciting, challenging and stimulating.

Since the fall of the Berlin Wall and the end of the cold war, RAF units have been engaged in successive operations in the Balkans, the Gulf and Afghanistan, and most recently over Libya. The moral complexities and pastoral consequences of these engagements have reinforced the need for chaplaincy. We have largely escaped the secularist pressures faced by some, finding instead that chaplains are in considerable demand from commanders, airmen and women, whether at training establishments or on operations.

The RAF Chaplains Branch is ecumenical in approach. However, all chaplains are expected to keep the integrity of their sending church. This united approach brings considerable support to a ministry that can sometimes feel isolated, either geographically or ecclesiastically. Our 'all souls' ministry also means that we are responsible for the care of those of all other faiths. On faith-specific issues we can refer individuals to, or gain advice from, one of the five civilian chaplains to the military, who represent the Hindu, Muslim, Buddhist, Jewish and Sikh faiths.

'Parish visiting' in RAF chaplaincy can involve patrolling with the regiment through an Afghan village, accompanying a Chinook crew in delivering troops to a forward position, collecting the injured, sharing a coffee in a crew room or having a quiet chat with an airwoman in a hangar. What is important is that we live out the Chaplain-in-Chief's vision of serving the whole RAF community through 'prayer, presence and proclamation'. Through prayer and presence we have earned the right to advise on moral and ethical matters both to senior leadership and junior ranks. Our accessibility demands that we be confident in who we are as priests and ministers and in what we have to offer to those living this demanding lifestyle.

Reference

Binyon, L. (1914; repr. 1984), from 'For the Fallen', in *The Oxford Book of War Poetry*, ed. J. Stallworthy. Oxford: Oxford University Press.

2

The Army

Stephen Robbins

If you observed a battle in the Middle Ages you would see the priests of the warring parties, on the edge of the battlefield, invoking God for the victory of their own troops and calling down curses on the other side. God was used as a weapon. Before the First World War, the cry from some chaplains was that our cause was just and God was on our side.

But in many ways the First World War changed all that. If God was on our side, why were we losing an average of 3,500 men a week? If God was on our side, why was a British soldier killed every three minutes? Easy theology doesn't work in this context, and to say 'God is on our side' or 'We are on God's side' is at best a delusion and at worst blasphemy. Chaplains and soldiers who witnessed the slaughter asked a valid theological question: 'What must God be like to let this happen?' The answer that one chaplain, Geoffrey Studdert Kennedy, gave is encapsulated in his 1919 book, *The Hardest Part*, a series of reflections on incidents in the trenches. Jürgen Moltmann said that it was the most important theological work published that year, which says a lot when you consider that 1919 also saw the publication of Karl Barth's *Epistle to the Romans*.

Studdert Kennedy's conclusion was that God is as he is in Jesus – not some eastern potentate sitting on a throne but the God who loves, the God who cares; the God who in Christ makes himself vulnerable for us and who on the cross suffers for and with his people in the context of and hope for the resurrection. In other words, the God who is love. It is this God of love who is the motivation for armed forces chaplaincy, as he is for all ministry. It is our calling, as we believe it is all Christians' calling, to love as he loved.

Armed forces personnel know something of love. They work together, live together, often socialize together. They face danger together, where they rely on one another for their very lives. They come to love one another. Some of the best examples of agape I have seen have been in the Army. What these people who know something of love are looking for from chaplains is to be loved by them, to be cared for by them and to be prayed for by them. This love of Christ that chaplains show is far more important to the troops than their denomination or whether they are catholic or evangelical. Love is more important than faith, and we can sometimes forget that.

Soldiers are not natural born killers and they often seek forgiveness for what they have done. I remember a corporal who asked his chaplain for Holy Communion. He had been out on patrol the night before and killed two of the enemy. He wanted to make his peace with God before going out again. Soldiers may not be queuing up at the altar rails but they do want the hope of resurrection when they are faced with their own death, or more importantly for them, the death of their friends. In the operating theatre in the hospital in Camp Bastion in Afghanistan, when a seriously injured soldier is brought in, the chaplain is in the theatre waiting as the surgical team does its job. If the patient dies, which sometimes happens, everything stops and the chaplain is called forward to say prayers. If we look at the tributes paid by the friends of those who have been killed, more often than not they include some religious references, such as 'I will see you on the other side' or 'RIP'.

Our unarmed chaplains face danger and face hardship to bring hope, a glimpse of heaven, to those caught up in hell. Army chaplains are there to give our officers and soldiers spiritual support, pastoral care and moral guidance.

Reference

Studdert Kennedy, G. A. (1919; repr. 2009), *The Hardest Part*. Charleston, SC: BiblioLife.

3

The Royal Navy

DAVID SIMPSON

'Good morning, are you here on religious business?' were the first words to me of a postdoc student as I arrived at the physics department coffee room. My retort was, 'Have you a confession to make?' Those words of introduction illustrate how far many chaplains in sector ministry have to travel in order to overcome the distance and role-projection that they encounter in their ministry. For many people the clerical collar suggests an ecclesiastical role that is about the Church as an institution, making it difficult for them to recognize that we may have other gifts, roles and ministries to offer. Ironically there can be as much to undo in perceptions of established church members as there is to build up for those who have no experience of the Church's ministry.

My reception on a Royal Navy warship is rather different. As the ship's chaplain crosses the gangway the quartermaster's greeting will more than likely be a wry smile and, 'Good morning, Bish, how are you?' 'Bish', short for 'bishop', of course, is a generic, colloquial term used of the chaplain by members of the Royal Navy. Others include 'Sin Bosun' and 'Sky Pilot'! Armed forces chaplains enjoy a profile and presence that is of the institution to which they belong. Each time chaplains stand up to speak in public they do so as part of a well-established service tradition. First impressions of chaplains are gained by trainee ratings and officer cadets in their initial training and carried on throughout their service career. If we stand up to speak at a memorial service for a Royal Marine killed in Afghanistan, offer a 'thought for the day' on the parade ground or say grace at a mess dinner, we refresh and revive our corporate presence in people's lives.

In doing so, we address the men and women with whom we share a rounded community life: three meals a day, military and physical exercise, life that can also involve sharing a cabin. Life in the Royal Navy is in some ways very levelling – the captain shares exactly the same risks as the ship's company; like the most junior sailor, he has to come to terms with long periods of separation from the support networks enjoyed at home and apply a range of technical and managerial skills 24/7 for as long as the ship is away. Chaplains are not protected from these emotional demands, so by their presence display solidarity in experiences that others are going through.

Imagine the scene in 2007. My ship was undergoing basic operational sea training in UK waters. The highlight of the week was the 'Thursday War', an exercise in which external assessors critique the ability of every-one, from the captain down, to fight and win a war. Living in a six-berth cabin with officer cadets, we secured our cabin for sea and had eaten breakfast by 0700. We were ready for a day of exercises that would involve operational activity: communications with other ships, tracking the threat of the enemy on the sea or in the air, helicopter sorties and proving our weapons systems. Those not involved in the ship's defensive or offensive role are spare hands doing damage control (preventing flooding as a result of enemy fire) and firefighting. As chaplain my role would be visiting the first-aid teams, providing moral support (often in the form of a packet of biscuits) for those wearied by long hours work-ing or waiting for something to happen, and being available to minister to those who might be dying of their wounds. Amid this exercise I was called to the bridge and asked to drive a sailor home to his family – a chance to support and befriend and be there in a time of real crisis.

Divided between work in seagoing appointments and shore establish-ments, a Royal Navy chaplain is described as 'the friend and adviser of all on board'. Unlike chaplains in the Army and the RAF, we carry no rank but adopt the rank of the person we're speaking to. (This is more an observation on the patterns of working of the other two services than a comment on their chaplaincies: Army and RAF chaplains wear 'relative' rank in order to access the rank-orientated structures of their services.) Not only is this an excellent way of illustrating our desire to 'be alongside' naval personnel, it says something about the radical values of the Kingdom of God we seek to promote: not needing authority over people, it enables us to speak with independence and moral authority.

What does this work mean sacramentally? At one level we are ourselves to be 'outward and visible signs of inward and spiritual grace' – available to others as signs and reminders of God's presence and work in every-day living, sharing the highs and lows. Naval chaplaincy must be second to none in its incarnational nature, in the tradition of the French worker-priests of the 1950s. Much of our role can be described as diaconal: helping the firefighting team put on their protective clothing, doing a morning with the chefs in the heat of the galley or arranging a visit to a battlefield site in the Falklands, sharing biscuits in the mess-deck and talking through the hopes and fears sailors feel at the end of a long period away from home.

Work of a priestly nature does arise, but in a very different form from that of parochial clergy. There can be requests for the baptism of a sailor's child – by tradition in the upturned ship's bell – and we can be asked to marry our people in a naval church. Every Sunday a ship is at sea there is an ecumenical service, and a small group may gather for the Eucharist or Bible study during the week. A distinctive aspect of this overt religious ministry is that it is integrated into a long-term relationship between the chaplain and the sailor. When so much of life is fragmented between work and leisure, being at home or away, sailors find that the ministry of the chaplain crosses boundaries, making him or her a natural confidante who is the only person on board who can (in accordance with a Ministry of Defence directive) offer absolute confidentiality. In this one-to-one work there is an element of being a reconciler, where the chaplain works to bring about a more constructive situation for the person concerned. I like to think of it as a form of spiritual direction in which, over time, faith issues can be explored and shared. Most importantly, all this is brought before God in a ministry of daily prayer and intercession.

In my experience of higher education chaplaincy, a large part of the work was finding a way into communities in which there was no natural role for a priest. Much rewarding work can be done there, but finding entrance was always the challenge. In the Royal Navy, the role is much clearer for all concerned. After that it's what we, and the Holy Spirit, make of it.

Part 2

CHAPLAINS' STORIES – EDUCATION

4

Durham School

ANNA DE LANGE

With a background in church administration and liturgy, rather than young people's work or pastoral care, it was something of a surprise when, in September 2002, I was asked to consider becoming chaplain to Durham School. I was aware even before I went for interview that I am very different from my predecessor. I am a Reader in the Church of England, a woman, and not a teacher. Moreover, I was to be part-time, continuing to live at home a mile or so away from school. 'Father Tim' had been an Anglican priest who taught religious studies as well as being chaplain. He had lived in a house belonging to the school and was employed full-time. One of the first issues I faced was what the pupils would call me. The 'father' model obviously did not fit, and I could not see myself as 'sister'! In the end I became 'Please, miss' to most of the young people, 'chaplain' to some and a rather diffident 'Anna' to a few I got to know well.

By the time I took up my duties the autumn term was well under way – I had to find my feet very quickly. There were chapel services to plan for the rest of the term and visiting speakers to be found, including Anglican clergy for the two occasions each term when our Friday service would be Holy Communion. But there was more. Four times a year, the first only three weeks away when I joined, the school hold their service in Durham Cathedral. It was up to me to put the service together, produce 500 service sheets, find pupils to take part, lead the service and liaise with the Cathedral. Moreover, the protocol of the Cathedral is that anyone leading such a service should take a final draft of the service to a meeting four weeks in advance. I had not started to think, I was already a week late, and the prospect of leading a service in Durham Cathedral was scary!

That first half-term was a baptism of fire but also a good way to get into the job. I made good use of those background skills I had thought irrelevant. Soon the pattern of planning services and speakers became familiar. Rotas and page layout were done quite easily. I worked out the best format for printing service sheets and began to forge contacts with excellent speakers. After Christmas I was able to turn my attention to my other main areas of responsibility: preparing any pupils who wanted to think about being confirmed, running a Christian Union or similar group and being available as a pastoral resource to both pupils and staff.

Durham School is a private co-educational school, about to break the 500 barrier for senior-school pupils. We have both boarders and day pupils and a long school day to allow a balance of lessons and a wide variety of sports, music, drama and other activities. Pupils arrive by 8.30 a.m. from a large area of the north-east, and even the youngest stay until at least 4.30 p.m. Many day pupils do not leave until 6.30 p.m. or later if they have evening rehearsals or matches.

The school chapel crouches like a cat at the top of a hill, overlooking the entire school site but rather separate from it. It is the only space large enough – just – to accommodate the whole school, and getting there involves climbing over 100 steps. Pupils make this journey for a 15-minute service three mornings a week and for a 45-minute service to close the week on Friday afternoon. There is no longer a chapel service on Sundays; boarders who wish to go to church are encouraged to visit one of the Durham parish churches.

So what, over the last eight years, have I learnt about the role? First, theologically, that above all the role is incarnational, representing God and things spiritual in a busy environment where it is not 'cool' to be a believer. The chaplain can draw alongside and support those among the community who do have faith, challenge those who do not and be a source of non-judgemental friendship to everyone. It has helped immensely that I do things that challenge stereotypes of what people expect a chaplain to be. My street-cred was improved no end when I started to run a rifle club and, at about the same time, arrived at school on a shiny new red motorbike.

Second, that this form of chaplaincy is a long and slow missional journey, sowing seeds rather than reaping harvests. Every chapel service is vitally important. Chapel is compulsory and, therefore, always full. However, many who are there have little or no Christian faith or experience. I ensure that in services we use 'we believe' (as a community) rather than 'I believe' (as an individual) language. The challenge is first to encourage them to listen and then to begin to think, even in a small and tentative way, about the possibility that there might be something in this 'God stuff' and about their place in the wider world. Sometimes individuals start to take further steps along the journey. Potential confirmation candidates are to be cherished, encouraged and challenged. This is to make sure that they want to take this first step in adult Christian discipleship for themselves, not just because someone else thinks it is time that they were 'done'.

Third, that for the pastoral role of a chaplain to work, you need regular contact with people. As a member of the staffroom I can do that with staff but as someone who does not teach it is difficult to get to know 500 pupils. It would be easier if I had enough hours to spend time being a minibus driver or a responsible adult for school trips. However, the wider pastoral structure of the school means that each pupil has access to a tutor, a housemaster/housemistress and the school nurse. It is still true, though, that when tragedy strikes, such as the sudden illness of a pupil or parent, the death of a loved grandparent or even of a dog, the simple act of writing and posting a card of sympathy is very much appreciated and opens doors to conversations.

In a busy school time is hard to find. A Christian Union after hours does not work for us. It is better to have a drop-in lunchtime discussion group over dinner trays. Similarly, confirmation groups need to be flexible and to fit around the inevitable games fixtures and concert rehearsals.

Last, it remains true that chapel ends up with a very special place in the hearts of even the most unlikely pupils. It is the part of school life that Old Dunelmians say they miss, even if they hated it while they were at school. Years after leaving, many want to have their marriage – and even funeral – services here.

I find myself being regarded as the 'vicar' of the school even though I am not ordained, but the joy is that I have no building to maintain, no PCC meetings and no funds to raise. On the other hand, I have to be my own churchwarden, secretary and verger. On a personal level I get my support from the church my husband and I go to on Sundays and from a termly meeting of diocesan youth workers.

After all that is said, my chief aim and vision is to help these young people, often so well-off in material terms but sometimes poor in spiritual, to think about the reality of God, the truth of Jesus and the things that make them tick. My hope is to set something running that may only come to fruition many years later. It matters not to me whether they come as atheists, agnostics, Anglicans, Roman Catholics, Muslims, Methodists or anything else. What matters is that they are all children of the God who loves them to bits and who wants them to know him better.

5

The Grey Coat Hospital and Westminster City School

GARRY SWINTON

While prominent within the school, chaplaincy in state schools often feels like a Cinderella ministry – barely noticed by diocesan authorities and little understood by others. I minister to nearly 2,000 students from 11 to 18 years old and almost 200 teachers and support staff. Unlike parish clergy I see most of my flock on a weekly basis, and many of them will be exposed to my teaching, assemblies or presence in and around the school. Some perhaps admire our work with awkward teenagers but few really understand the significance of what we do and the impact we might have on shaping the future of the Church. While there are national officers in the Church of England responsible for promoting and supporting other chaplaincies, state school chaplains often work alone in terms of the wider Church.

My duties exercise both my vocations. As both an ordained priest and qualified teacher, there is always the need to protect one's role as the priest from those who write timetables for the teacher! My own salary is partly paid by the trustees of the schools. I sometimes have to remind colleagues I am neither a cover teacher nor a full member of a subject department.

I teach half-time and also take responsibility for collective worship (assemblies) as well as church services for major festivals and special occasions in the school year. There are many other roles but in all I do I am involved in nurturing the religious ethos of both schools. In church schools the chaplain is the guardian of the religious ethos, under the leadership of the head teacher and governors. Where church membership is frequently not an essential qualification for students and other members of staff, we are expected to show how a church school is distinctive.

Collective worship is the core of the chaplain's work. We must model good practice not only because the students, as a captive audience, deserve it but because other colleagues look to you as the one who should be the expert. Within the classroom, and in collective worship, a chaplain must be able to guide impressionable minds and be a liturgical inter-preter of life in school and the world they are to inherit. We are their prophet and pastor in times of crisis, death, violence and tragedy. We are their celebrant in times of rejoicing.

As a teacher, time is caught up in lesson preparation, which never lessens as benchmarks rise. Being a teacher also means managing behaviour and dealing, at times, with unfocused and restless students. I have to balance the tasks of maintaining discipline and loving teenagers into heaven. Frequently I use Genesis to remind colleagues that our students are made in the image of God, even if at times that image is blurred! Chaplaincy is about searching for that image – as well as writing reports about academic progress.

Religious belief is a mixed-ability activity. Ask any group of students – from the 'gifted and talented' to those with 'special needs' – to draw up a list of big questions about life and death and the list will basically be the same. Young people, whatever grown-ups think, care about their world – about war and poverty, about those caught up in natural and human disasters – and they care about each other. The news headlines are shaped, in one form or another, by religious politics and diversity. The importance of equipping young people – for whom religious questions are a serious concern – to begin to address them should never be underestimated.

While wrestling with those big questions, the chaplain has a unique contribution to make. Moses took the ancient Israelites from captivity in Egypt into the wild place en route to the Promised Land. It was on this journey that the identity of God's people was formed. It is important that the chaplain, as one who regularly stands in front of students to deliver assemblies, should recognize this and address issues, images and questions that resonate with young people. They are often in a wild place and, in their confusion, they so easily latch on to certainties in their search for stability. Our calling is to assist them in working out a credible, critical and sustainable theology and spirituality.

Jesus asked, 'Who do people say that I am?' (Mark 8.27). The question of identity is a central issue in the life of every teenager. They are often confused, vulnerable and sometimes angry as they try to make sense of themselves and the muddles in the world. A state-school chaplain will inevitably deal with those whose parents care and those who do not. Some may be injured in some way and, together with the school, the chaplain must bring the injured for healing. Just as Jesus fuelled the fun at Cana, the chaplain must also be able to show that God affirms life and has a sense of humour.

In all things our ministry must be unconditional, non-judgemental, open-minded and able to value the spiritual tradition of others in a non-partisan way. In the Gospels, Jesus embraced all, not just those who belonged. William Temple highlighted the essence of Anglicanism when he said, 'The Church is the only society that exists for the benefit of those who are not its members.' The strength of the Anglican Church is its role as the nation's pastor and priest. We are called, with all its challenges, to minister to everyone.

In many schools, including my own, we teach students and recruit staff from a range of Christian denominations and other faiths or no faith. The essential requirement is that they support our ethos. My own schools reflect the diversity of London, taking students from all the major Christian denominations and world faiths. In one of my schools students come from over 50 national backgrounds; in the other it's 90.

The chaplain must be able to embrace the stranger and see ministry as moving from Babel to Pentecost. I took up my own position in September 2001, days before the tragedy of September 11. I work with many articulate, reflective and committed members of other faiths. My ministry is one of promoting dialogue and understanding in a non-threatening place. On a couple of occasions in Ramadan I have felt affirmed when Muslim students expected me as the 'holy man' to fast in solidarity with them! It is about creating a place where teenagers educate each other about their religious practices.

Death is perhaps the most shocking part of my work. As I took up my post I anticipated a range of experiences in terms of the occasional offices. Burying a student was something I had not expected and, when the first of four deaths came, I felt ill-prepared for what happened. Student death is always tragic. My own experiences have been deaths from natural causes but other colleagues have dealt with road accidents and with those caught up in knife and gang crime. Whatever the cause, however anticipated the death might be, it will always be a shock in a school community. It turns upside down the cycle of nature and challenges our theological view of the world. Ironically, these occasions are also opportunities when the ministry of the chaplain is most obvious, valued, needed and essential. For students and colleagues within the school, the chaplain becomes, at that moment, the one who is most equipped to face the crisis.

Death has to be dealt with directly and should be discussed in its rawness. Teenagers have the ability to deal with the issue with greater fortitude and resilience than grown-ups often give them credit for. When a student dies, the chaplain's routine is suspended in order to liaise with the student's family and church congregation, while at the same time managing the grief of a whole school community. This is exhausting and demanding.

This is my ministry and these are my circumstances. Other school chaplains will have different ones. What joins us together is the recognition that teenagers are scary, because they speak their mind. They are sophisticated because they live in the age of iPhones and the Internet, PowerPoint and Prezi. They are beyond the chalk and talk on which many of us were brought up. The challenges they bring are enormous and yet they teach and inspire us.

6

A further-education college

Clare McBeath

It was one of the childcare tutors who first drew my attention to Chantelle. She was late with assignments and had stormed out of class. Moreover, she had mentioned a forthcoming court appearance. 'Could I possibly come over and meet with her – now!' She looked half starved, sleep-deprived and dishevelled, street-wise but very vulnerable.

So began a lengthy and heart-wrenching journey of walking with Chantelle during her two years at college. Chantelle was 17. My first meeting with her barely scratched the surface in terms of the multiplicity of needs she embodied. We went to the court appearance together, an application for access arrangements to visit her child who was in the care of social services. I went with her to meetings with social services and, eventually, to visit her in a mother and baby assessment unit. I learnt that her parents were drug users and that her former partner, aged 35 (Chantelle would have been 15), was violent, in prison, and the reason the baby was in care. I walked with her as she presented at Women's Direct Access and moved in to various hostels. All ended in eviction due to an ongoing cannabis habit. Barely a month would go by without some new crisis looming. If I could have done so, I would have been tempted to take her home and foster her myself. That is what she desperately needed, except that she would have been a self-destructive nightmare.

While her case is on the extreme end of a spectrum, she was by no means unusual. Why put all that energy and time into the Chantelles of further education? Because, underneath it all, I believed that she was made in God's image, that God loved her and that she was very much the victim of the total mess of the world the adults around her had made.

Did we ever talk about faith? Yes, once and in depth. It was the week before Christmas. We sat over coffee, Coke and sandwiches and she asked why I bothered with her when she kept making such a mess of everything. I told her a story of an unmarried teenager who heard voices, got herself pregnant, was homeless, had a baby in a stable and then had to flee the authorities. I think it was the first time she had really heard the Christmas story and seen the connections with her own life.

The context in which I worked was one of the largest further-education colleges in the country, delivering most of a northern industrial city's sixth form, vocational and adult education courses, including English for speakers of other languages (ESOL). The number of sites changed constantly but at one point numbered over 20 across the city. According to the index of multiple deprivation, the city itself ranks as one of the most deprived in the country.

The chaplaincy was multi-faith, consisting of one full-time post, job-shared between me and a colleague, also a Christian. There was no counselling service but there was a small support team of mainly careers advisers and one of youth workers with whom we worked closely. As a chaplaincy we were very much a drop in a vast ocean. When I started I had assumed that the only viable way of developing the multi-faith chaplaincy was to engage volunteers from different faiths and covering different parts of the city. Unfortunately, I was told that the institution would not be able to quality-control or line-manage volunteers.

So what did the job involve? Mainly crisis response! Having thrown up my hands in horror at the antiquated pager I was given, I acquired a mobile phone and an email address. This at least enabled us to adopt a kind of triage system based on how urgent a request was. We divided up the sites between us. However, this did not work if a crisis occurred on my colleague's patch on his or her day off.

We dealt with emergencies ranging from student deaths, serious illnesses, child protection, mental-health issues, suspected pregnancies and domestic abuse, to the less urgent but nevertheless real issues of bereavement, sexuality, accommodation, the criminal justice system, finance, drugs/alcohol, asylum applications and forced marriages, to list but some. Very occasionally students did come to us with issues of faith, but usually complicated by some practical problem such as being Muslim and coming out as homosexual, or Roman Catholic and coming to terms with abuse within the Church.

Each visit had to be written up with actions for follow-up, usually telephone calls and subsequent visits. Sometimes we would only see a student once; often it was several times over the course of a few weeks; occasionally it was regular or crisis visits over a longer period of time.

The chaplaincy was specifically for students and not for staff. Nevertheless staff did come to us with issues, particularly around their own faith, and we did hold regular lunchtime prayer/reflections. It was often these members of staff who were the greatest advocates of chaplaincy and who made the most referrals.

Other roles included attending student inductions, maintaining chaplaincy notice boards and prayer rooms and delivering occasional tutorials. We held events at some of the major festivals. At certain times we held reflections on world events, such as the 2004 tsunami or for black history month. Occasionally we provided mediation. Some of the issues we picked up were site- or course-specific. For example, the Roman Catholic sixth form had a high number of suspected pregnancies, so we engaged Brook, the local teenage sexual health service, to do some tutorials. The adult education centres occasionally had issues of timing courses around Muslim prayer or Ramadan fasts.

In the Ofsted inspection shortly after I left, the college was awarded an 'outstanding' and the work of the chaplaincy was highlighted. So why did I leave? Quite simply because after only two years part-time I recognized the signs of impending burn-out. It was not that I did not try to put in place the support I needed, but the college refused to pay for supervision for the heavy caseload I was carrying. There was a real sense of isolation and a lack of professional development or networking opportunities – nor had a clear rationale for chaplaincy even been laid down. Partly this was because the institution did not see its importance and partly because the various denominations do not really have a category for further-education chaplaincy. Churches often include it within university chaplaincy when really it is quite different.

Every time we tried to develop the chaplaincy to tackle some of the more strategic issues students were facing, or tried to network with other agencies that could help, it was questioned. I guess, in a nutshell, that I saw the chaplaincy as needing to be engaged at a strategic level within the college and local community rather than at the bottom of the line-management chain – to be proactive as well as reactive. This is borne out by the subsequent governance and chairing roles in the public/voluntary sectors I have taken on as a local Baptist minister working in the inner city to address some of the issues of deprivation.

So what is the role of chaplaincy within further education? For me, the best description I can come up with is that of 'walking with people in pain' and of 'signposting' people to others on their journey who may be able to help. I often felt I was at the connection of a huge hub of networks of agencies and organizations. Without them, the job would have been undoable and I would have been of little help to many students.

In theological language it is an incarnational ministry, a ministry of journeying with and holding people in pain and helping them to move on. I may not have had a lot of conversations specifically about faith, partly because the students I worked with did not have the luxury of time and affluence to reflect deeply on faith issues but were struggling to survive and get through each day. However, in a very real sense I felt as though I were walking in the footsteps of Jesus in his ministry, in a ministry that all too often led right to the foot of the cross. Just occasionally I got to glimpse resurrection!

7

Sunderland University

STEPHEN FAGBEMI

My position at the University of Sunderland is a full-time post created within the team of clergy working at Sunderland Minster. This means that I have some responsibilities for taking services and preaching at the Minster as arranged by rota with other colleagues. At Sunderland the Anglican chaplain is the only full-time chaplain and so has responsibilities for running the chaplaincy and providing leadership for the multi-faith team. Here these include the Islamic imam, Jewish rabbi, Methodist minister, Roman Catholic priest and Sikh guru among others. This requires a broad-minded individual who is experienced and skilled in both ecumenical and interfaith relations.

As a team of chaplains, our responsibility is to provide pastoral, religious and social support for all people in the university. In other words, we are primarily concerned about people's well-being. The chaplaincy has a holistic approach to ministry to both staff and students. We encourage staff members to practise their faith in the workplace by providing the enabling environment for that to happen. The same goes for students, whose entire life centres on the university during the period of their studies. This holistic approach means that there is a strong welfare aspect to what we do. The chaplain has a duty of care and is responsible for some of the provision of social opportunities for students, many of whom will have recently left home for the first time or have come from abroad. Accordingly we not only concentrate on prayer and worship or Bible teaching but also engage in many social activities and involve students in current affairs. We are here to support people's growth and spiritual journeys.

The UK continues to have a changing view of the essence of what a university is for. While universities continue to pursue vigorously the research and academic agenda, changing government policies continue to reshape them. There is an ongoing debate over whether universities are primarily for business enterprise or education. Put differently, the question might be whether universities are equipping people for the future world outside the academic environment. In my view, this way of posing the question encompasses both education and enterprise. Real education helps to raise the right questions and equips one to face them in the long run. Thus our task is ultimately the holistic development of individuals, equipping them to face the world. This is where the role of chaplaincy is vital. As Newman (2006) said, university is not simply a place to acquire head knowledge. It is much more a place to develop the total person, including the spiritual, emotional, social and academic constituents of the human being. The chaplain makes a major contribution to this, even if that contribution is not often well acknowledged.

So this is a very broad role. On many occasions I engage in things that do not have any direct bearing on religion but rather are issues of support more generally. I believe people greatly appreciate this broad and holistic approach. With students we hold weekly meetings for Christian discussion and fellowship. We also run a variety of social events to enable interaction and relationships with those of other faiths or none. I also support other religious societies and, through the associate chaplains and faith advisers, ensure that the different religious groups are adequately supported.

I interact with staff in many and diverse ways. Simply by going around the university I engage in all sorts of discussions. Through this I am able to offer support and encouragement while also creating friendships. I am privileged to listen to people's concerns and fears as well as the joys and successes they would like to share, while I offer them prayers or any other suitable support. Sometimes I am called by people in desperate need of intervention, advice or help – they often consider the chaplaincy the only point of call for non-prejudicial support. A chaplain has a degree of independence, especially when not being paid or only partly being paid by the university. This means that he or she is able to deal with issues without any fear, able to offer support to people who may have a problem with the university. The independent nature of the chaplaincy is vital in that we are able to challenge the university authorities if we notice issues of concern.

I also engage in diversity and ethical matters, encourage involvement in charity and act as an interface between the university and the city. Community links and widening participation mean that the university is constantly engaged with the city and its strategy. This developed initially from the city's recognition of the university as a significant partner and player in the local economy. Now the chaplains work closely with the city on interfaith matters and matters relevant to helping the growth of a lively multicultural city. For example, we organize Christmas hospitality for international students to enjoy Christmas dinner with local families, thereby facilitating friendship between local people and university students. I currently chair the

Sunderland Interfaith Forum. This is aimed at bringing people of different faiths together, not only so that they might understand each other and live peaceably but also to facilitate their contributions to the Sunderland strategy and its delivery.

As a priest, I also provide an interface between church and university. The challenge here is to maintain a balance between the social and spiritual aspects of ministry. In my experience, the pressure on universities to be more attractive to people of different ethnic backgrounds and faiths is transferred to the chaplain, who has to provide for the wide variety of needs of people of different backgrounds and faiths. It is in this engagement that I have often found exciting opportunities to minister and deal with spiritual issues.

Yet the ministry of the chaplain as a priest within a worshipping community also requires articulation. For me personally, this side of ministry finds expression through my interaction with university staff members when we meet to pray and study. There is much delight in opportunities to host major services such as the university Christmas carol service or the All Souls' Day memorial service that take place at the Minster. However, it is in the other part of my ministry, as chaplain to Sunderland Minster, that my priestly duties find the greatest expression. This includes being part of a team of clergy who meet to pray and discuss pastoral and ministry-related matters and who take turns to perform other duties such as preaching, leading prayer and healing services, presiding at Holy Communion and taking weddings, baptisms and funerals.

In conclusion, being a chaplain in a new university poses all kinds of challenges, including the flexible nature of the role, especially when the chaplain is performing non-conventional priestly tasks. But the importance of the job is appreciated anew in meeting with, being available to and offering support to lonely and sometimes desperate individuals. It is in the commitment of the chaplain to a Christ-centred ministry that other daily tasks find meaning. In such contexts I find that theology becomes more creative and mission more interesting.

Reference

Newman, J. H. (2006), *The Idea of a University*. London: Baronius Press.

8

Sheffield Hallam University

IAN MAHER

Since January 2006 it has been my privilege to lead a multi-faith chaplaincy team drawn from 14 different religious traditions. Our faith advisers are all volunteers, my own full-time university-funded post being the only stipendiary appointment. The chaplaincy offers pastoral support to students and staff of all faiths and none, provides religious advice and guidance across the university and works to promote greater awareness of religious needs and sensitivities within the institution.

Our base in the university is a multi-faith centre that was opened in November 2007. The centre incorporates the chaplaincy office, a quiet room, two general-purpose meeting rooms as well as Muslim prayer rooms (male and female). My role includes the management of this space.

Working in such a diverse religious context and within such a rainbow team of faith advisers is an immensely enriching experience but one that inevitably challenges assumptions and stereotypes about religious belief and practice. Certainly one of the most satisfying aspects of the post is helping students from different faith backgrounds to meet each other and begin to appreciate each other's beliefs, perhaps for the first time. This is not always easy but the benefits more than repay the effort.

However, and not surprisingly, tensions arise from time to time within the university environment, where the ethos is predominantly secular. Occasionally the question is raised, albeit implicitly: 'What place does religion have in a secular institution?' This reflects a misplaced assumption that a person's religion can be left at the door, and betrays a distorted understanding of what it means to be religious. Thankfully there is now wider acceptance of the need to respect and value the insights and contribution of people of faith. This has been helped considerably by the incorporation of issues of religion and belief within the broader equality-and-diversity agenda.

One misconception relating to religious provision within the university is that it has to be equal across all religions. This is not the case, for the simple reason that the needs of different religions vary. For example, designated prayer space is important to Muslims but not in the same way to Christians. Recognizing that equal respect does not equate to identical provision makes practical responses to religious needs on campus more realistic and achievable. The insight and expertise with which the university is provided by the broad religious representation within the chaplaincy team is invaluable in this respect.

Despite this, one difficult and ongoing challenge is the indifference, apathy and occasionally even hostility that is present towards organized religion generally. For many, religion is seen as irrelevant, which helps explain why events and initiatives offered by the chaplaincy sometimes elicit relatively low response rates. In contrast there is much greater engagement with the broader concepts of spirituality and well-being. Religions have much to say in relation to such concepts, and that is proving a more fruitful approach in terms of making connections between chaplaincy and those who do not profess a religious affiliation.

There are many joys in the role I occupy but three in particular stand out. First, the humbling experience of standing alongside and walking a little way with students who share deeply personal concerns. I am not sure that the public at large are really aware of the particular and considerable pressures faced by young people at university in these trying times. My own eyes have certainly been opened since taking up this post. Relationships, finance, accommodation, academic demands and family concerns are just some of the things that can come together during the university years and create a 'perfect storm' for a student.

Second, there are lots of opportunities, formal and informal, to facilitate positive encounters between students from different religions and also between religious and non-religious students. Universities are places from which many of the movers and shakers of the world in the immediate future will emerge, so fostering the ability to engage critically while respecting different views and beliefs is arguably no less a significant outcome for universities than the achievement of academic excellence. It is immensely satisfying to feel that the multi-faith chaplaincy is able to contribute in some small way to helping students both respect and value diverse beliefs and practices.

Third, there is the experience of working in a team that encompasses what on paper would seem to be an impossible amount of religious and theological difference. Our life together is sustainable through the mutual recognition of each other's integrity and the simultaneous acknowledge-ment that on some things we must agree to differ. This does not mean stifling legitimate debate and discussion but, rather, being realistic about what should and should not take up our time. For example, if Christians and Muslims have argued about the nature of Christ for 1,400 years, it is hardly likely that we will resolve the matter at Sheffield Hallam. Instead we focus on concerns held in common on which we can engage together: working to help ensure that a person's religion is taken seriously and respected within the university; collaborating to meet the particular spiritual needs of our students and staff; countering negative stereotypes of religion.

Where, you might ask, does Christian mission and ministry find expression within such a complex setting? This is a particularly pointed question for me as a member of the Church Army, an Anglican society of evangelists, but one not as difficult to answer as it might seem.

First and foremost in this context, mission is incarnational. Being present and available to students and staff, whether for one-to-one meetings, group discussion or through involvement in committees and networks, creates opportunities for a Christian perspective to be brought to bear. The same is, of course, true for any Christians studying or working at university, though my identification with the chaplaincy heightens this awareness.

Working in partnership with other student support services, such as counselling, education guidance and the mental-health service, also witnesses to the fact that the Christian gospel is concerned about a person's wholeness of life and thereby reflects the longing of Jesus that we might have fullness of life.

Another aspect of mission is that of service. The chaplaincy is often to be found 'working in the gaps'; in other words, being a first contact-point for students who have perhaps fallen between other support services or for whom staff members have not been able to clarify a specific need. What we offer is time and a listening ear. Sometimes that is all that is needed, or it may be the beginning of helping a student to explore the issues in question, religious or otherwise. At other times chaplaincy is something of a triage point from which we direct students to other avenues of support.

If there were one word to describe the nature of Christian mission in this context, it would be 'messy'. Things are seldom neat and tidy and often our work is more about helping people to live with the tough questions than offering glib answers. That makes it difficult to conform to the strongly results-focused approach that runs throughout the higher-education sector, leaving chaplaincy standing in a potentially vulnerable place in a climate of financial constraints and cuts. That said, being in a place of service and vulnerability has some clear resonance with the life and ministry of Jesus. Certainly for those of us who are Christians within the chaplaincy, that is a source of great encouragement in the practical outworking of our Christian discipleship.

Holding the tension between maintaining the integrity of being a follower of a particular religion, while genuinely open to the contribution of colleagues of different faith traditions, is an important task in any multi-faith chaplaincy context and particularly so for the coordinator/leader. This is not always easy and can be frustrating when some things take much longer to work through than they would in a single-faith team. But the fruits of multi-faith chaplaincy far outweigh any downside.

9

Selwyn and Newnham Colleges, Cambridge

HUGH SHILSON-THOMAS

My first experience of university chaplaincy was as a student, and it was at university that my vocation to ordained ministry was nurtured. Conversations with the chaplain were significant in helping me believe that ministry might indeed be my calling. After a period as a lay assistant in Liverpool – where again I saw chaplains at work – and curacies in two parishes in south-east London, becoming a university chaplain felt like a natural progression.

My first appointment was at a polytechnic in south-west London. I had barely arrived before the polytechnic became a university. This is symptomatic of the pace of life in modern universities. Student communities turn over very quickly – three years is a generation, and that presents a real challenge to those whose ministerial formation has been in a more traditional parish.

When I came to leave this large university – on four sites with some 16,000 students – for a college in Cambridge with just a few hundred, it was not for a rest; but it was a change. The former polytechnic had no dedicated sacred space. Classrooms were booked out by me for Islamic prayers and the mid-week Communion. Although more people apologized for not being able to come to the Communion services than ever actually came, people knew this informed what I did. A chaplain can be there for everyone but cannot be all things to everyone. While a Christian minister can work ecumenically, in an interfaith way and even in a multi-faith chaplaincy, in my view the term 'multi-faith chaplain' is highly problematic. Vice-chancellors want efficiency. One person for all sounds appealing. Yet in order to speak to others' traditions with credibility it is necessary to be rooted in one's own.

The challenge in my former context was how to engage with ministry to the institution. In my subsequent working with chaplains across the country it became clear that this is now a feature of chaplaincy work in the majority of British universities. Their sheer size necessitates working within the structures, forging institutional relationships that enable pastoral interactions that in turn allow questions of faith to be brought to the surface and aired legitimately in a context in which overt proselytism may be discouraged or forbidden. Universities are essentially private institutions. It is increasingly difficult for anyone to wander in to them to meet students or seek to influence them. Consequently, for the benefit of institutions, student communities and faith communities it is vital to preserve relationships of trust that have been built up by chaplains over many years. These relationships are hard won and easily lost.

Where there are few opportunities for gathering people together, a chaplain has to go to where the people are and get to know them in their own contexts. This incarnational approach to ministry seems entirely fitting. An opportunity once arose, for example, to curate a show in the faculty of art. I did not know much about art. However, the students did know why they were painting and sculpting the way they were. Encouraging them to think about the ways their faith and world-view was being expressed and communicated was exciting.

In a fairly benign, generally disinterested though occasionally hostile community, not having a chapel to worry about had the great advantage of not giving others the opportunity to think that that was where I ought to be. However, after five years I felt the lack of a church or chapel. So often opportunities to preach in local churches were motivated by the need for cover, rather than the desire to hear about what was going on in the university. Unfortunately many churches still see their relationship with students as being primarily about bringing students into their church buildings. Where young people are not going to church, the opportunity for the church to go to them needs to be valued. I have come to understand my role as a chaplain as working in the university on behalf of the Church outside it.

The difference in Cambridge has been in the level of awareness of chaplaincy and the increased potential to engage significantly with the lives of many people, whether or not they go to church. In a relatively small institution the chaplain has the potential to know everyone's name and can work with a much greater proportion of the community. People see the chapel as 'their' chapel and the chaplain as 'their' chaplain, even if they are not Christians. My experience is that students have to be highly motivated to knock on a chaplain's door to discuss a matter of faith or a personal crisis of some kind, which is how many discussions of faith actually start. They are most likely to do so if one of their peers, whom they trust, speaks of knowing the chaplain.

Here students are resident. They go out into the wider university for some lectures and classes but come back to the college for other teaching and also to eat, sleep and study. A chaplain in this sort of college ministers to people in their work and leisure time. Someone once told me that, in answer to a question about how to be a good chaplain, a wise colleague responded, 'Walk slowly.' In college people meet each other regularly. There are shared spaces – the dining hall, cafeteria, bar, chapel, common rooms – where all college members are entitled to be, whether undergraduates, postgraduates, staff or chaplains. While it is not easy to 'walk slowly', I am convinced that good chaplaincy is about leaving space between things that provides opportunities for conversations that might not otherwise happen.

Theologically the Pauline texts about common membership of the one body, each member exercising its different function, have much to say to colleges. We use 'body' language a great deal – student body, governing body, senior and junior members, for example. Colleges are self-consciously communities, and it is that sense of common belonging that facilitates conversation (literally, 'turning with') and enables the exploration of values and the sharing of ideas and beliefs. In a university we are engaged in the common enterprise of discerning what to think and what to believe. Ongoing conversations are possible in a college – albeit over a limited period – because of the relative ease of identifying both the chaplains and those who have a faith. This was not nearly as easy in my former, larger, institutional chaplaincy, where I was once asked if I was really a priest or just dressed like one.

In colleges with Christian foundations the Church has a particular resource. Here Christian presence should not have to be argued for and chaplains are relatively secure. As someone engaged in ministry I view them as relatively small and well-resourced parishes, just as larger universities may be different sorts of parishes. If parish ministry is about being where the people are (historically where they lived, worked and spent their leisure time), then universities are modern-day parishes. There is widespread misunderstanding about this. Chaplains are criticized for 'leaving parish ministry', as if their vocation is undermined by the move. Sadly college chaplains are sometimes criticized by other clergy for leaving the mainstream and taking what is perceived to be an easier option. All ministry is challenging in its various contexts; we are all in the same 'business'. With 44 per cent of people aged between 17 and 30 entering higher education, it seems self-evident that this is where the Church needs to be.

As chaplains we must recognize the vital work we are entrusted with: serving the people who inhabit the world of higher education and making connections in the institution between the life of faith and the life of the university, and between the university and the community of faith. In higher education lives are transformed. Paul's invocation to 'be transformed by the renewing of your minds' (Romans 12.2) reminds me of the vital importance of the educational endeavour and of the

Church's place in it. As a chaplain the importance of this task has kept me going when the road has seemed lonely or overwhelming. When the business culture of modern higher education tends to focus on evidence of results, the observation (drafted by Bishop Untener for a homily spoken by Cardinal Dearden and often wrongly attributed to Oscar Romero) that 'We plant seeds that one day will grow' has reassured me of the importance of the journey and the need to take the long view.

10

King's College London

Jane Speck

A room in which to do chaplaincy work is a precious thing (Virginia Woolf would understand) and is something many chaplains have to do without. I am one of the lucky ones. Here the chaplaincy team is blessed with the support of the college to the extent that we have dedicated chaplaincy space on each of the college's four main sites around London. The chaplaincy team consists of one full-time and three part-time Anglican chaplains, part-time Orthodox, Roman Catholic and Free Church chaplains, links to the Jewish chaplain for the south-east and two full-time chaplaincy assistants.

Of course, with space comes responsibility. Today, at the end of an exceptionally full year, I am at King's Waterloo site making a note of the room's wear and tear so that I can put in my annual deep-clean request. As I do so, I find myself thinking about how it all happened. Stains, scuffs and litter may be an odd way to remember the year but it reflects the gloriously down-to-earth nature of so much of our work.

I have a lovely deep-blue carpet which, throughout the year, gets gradually obscured. The latest stains look suspiciously like trodden-in meringue from last week's Pimms and Strawberries party. Several students got excited about creating creamy-meringuey-strawberry-y puddings, laced with Pimms, which went down a storm. Under the meringue is an assortment of ground-in crumbs from a year of international lunches. Sometimes 4, sometimes 40 students, from China to Poland to the USA and beyond, cram themselves into the room every Tuesday for free food, lots of chatter and, for some, a safe refuge amid a demanding, complicated and confusing college life.

There are the coffee splashes on the walls – I have no idea how they got there – and chips in the paintwork that need touching up. In a room without windows (the blessing of space only goes so far in an institution where every square inch is fought for) I went for cosy terracotta paint. It seems to me that a beautiful space is an important part of the warm welcome we offer. Universities are places of hard lines, uncomfortable chairs and functional space. To have a 'living room' immediately sets us apart and gives the people who come here permission to let go and let be. I have noticed this year that more and more students are using this room to work, preferring the relaxed atmosphere here to the tense stress of the library.

In the corner the pile for recycling is getting bigger. Flattened teabag boxes form the bulk of it. We get through ridiculous amounts of the regular sort but for some we order specially. Raspberry leaf for a Quaker with a wicked sense of humour and too much energy to be safe with caffeine. Redbush for a member of staff who came to chaplaincy through the confirmation classes, over the months joined us in meditation, weekly prayer and Eucharists, then invited me to take her wedding in chapel last month. Earl Grey for the welfare officer and senior tutor who drop in with student referrals and the latest news on students whose care we have shared.

Then there is the stack of empty tissue boxes. There are the random callers who burst into tears the moment they are asked, 'How're things?' They pour out their stories, receive prayer and, if fitting, practical advice; then, often as not, they disappear back into college life. Then there are the regular visitors who take time to trust, to decide whether to open up. And there are those I do not see, those who visit the chaplaincy assistant or come in to clean at night then stay a while, telling me later how they sit and pour out their troubles and tears to the icon of Christ propped up on the table.

We have got through a lot of washing-up-liquid bottles too. Masses of cups and plates have taken up hours of the chaplaincy assistant's time. Chaplaincy assistants come to us for a year. It's an opportunity to think about their own sense of calling and to experience the grittier side of ministry. They do a lot of shopping and washing up and are amazingly supportive in the way they free us to do other things. This year the assistant spent half the year struggling stubbornly and at times painfully to put together new shoe racks for the sisters' side of our Muslim prayer room. The time he put into making them helped build relationships with the people who use the room. We just did not expect to get through three screwdriver sets to assemble them!

All the throws, tablecloths and cushion covers need to be washed. As I bundle them up I think about the student who will curl up and sleep whenever the room is quiet; the night cleaners who kip here during their shifts; the members of the Women's Network gathering to plan meetings; the candlelit prayer meetings that soak the very walls in prayer. Some stains you just do not want to remove.

When I reflect theologically about what I do in chaplaincy I think about Jesus getting his hands dirty; eating, travelling, weeping with people. He gave people what they needed, whether time, food, prayer or teaching. If I seek to follow him, why try to do my chaplaincy work any differently?

People often ask whether I would like to get back into full-time parish ministry or try another form of chaplaincy. I have wondered too over the last year, eventually narrowing my preferred options down to hospice chaplaincy, diocesan director of ordinands or retraining as a psychotherapist. Then I had one of those mornings when there was nothing in the diary and nothing pressing to do. I was tempted to skive but a distressed member of staff walked through the door – her father was dying. She specifically wanted to know, 'What's it like to be with someone when they die?' I pulled my experience in hospice ministry to the fore and we talked. After she had gone another member of staff phoned to see if she could pop over; she thought she might be called to some form of ministry. We had a long chat about vocations and agreed how she might move forward. Being only half-time I was then getting ready to go back to the parish when a student slipped silently around the door. She has recently been diagnosed with schizophrenia and is terrified that this will force an end to her future in medicine. For an hour I listen, encourage and do what I can to share the burden of her fear.

There they were, in one morning, all the aspects of ministry I thought I might need to choose between. University chaplaincy gives me all of these and more. I have the privilege of forming Christian community and meeting/working with people who have nothing to do with the Church. I get to work pastorally with a huge range of staff and students. I get invited to teach, occasionally, on spirituality, difference or aspects of faith. I am paid to hang out with people, drinking coffee and laughing. As cuts hit higher education I am called on to support both people whose jobs are threatened and those who have to make the difficult decisions. I celebrate Eucharists, lead meditations, look after the Muslim prayer room and provide for other religious societies and individuals who need space to practise their faith.

If there are tensions for me in this work they are mostly about time and opportunity. With just 20 hours a week I am constantly making hard decisions about where and with whom I should be. Some years I seem to spend all my time with staff, out and about in the college; others it feels like I have never left the office and the groups of students hanging out there. Always I feel as though I need to be where I am *and* somewhere else. As a consequence it is easy to end up living with a permanent sense of unspecified failure. It is vital to me to have days like today when I remember what has been achieved in a year. The beauty of the room is not, ultimately, in the decor but in the stains left on the floor and on my soul. The last thing a chaplaincy room should be is a hideaway in which I hole up and hope that people will come to me. It needs, rather, to be a place where we can all find nurturing and rejuvenation, finding the strength to go out into the college, community and world.

Part 3

CHAPLAINS' STORIES – HEALTHCARE

11

Rotherham NHS Foundation Trust

Joan Ashton

I am privileged to be a healthcare chaplain and I believe it is the ministry to which God has called and equipped me. It is a role from which I daily derive great joy and confirmation of my calling. Both joyful and painful, it is a ministry that often leaves me humbled by the resilience of the human spirit in the face of chronic illness and death, and by the willingness of patients to share deep feelings, fears and spiritual pain.

My initial interest in hospital chaplaincy began through a placement in a local hospital as part of pre-ordination training. I had a sense that this could be a ministry into which, at some future point, I might be called. Sadly, within post-ordination training there were no opportunities to explore this further. Only when I was appointed to my first parish was I able to make contact with the nearest hospital and explore chaplaincy more deeply, becoming a volunteer chaplain. Within a short space of time I moved into a dual-role ministry, priest in charge of a small parish and also half-time assistant chaplain at the nearby hospital. This proved an ideal setting in which to discern whether my future calling was to parish or hospital ministry.

The five years that I spent in this dual role meant that I worked for two very different large organizations – the hospital and the diocese. My parish ministry operated on a traditional model of church and its mission of witnessing and serving those who lived within the parish boundary. By contrast, as a chaplain my work was spread across all wards and departments of the hospital and demanded a much more flexible approach, requiring the ability to respond quickly and effectively to urgent requests for spiritual care in traumatic, often unexpected, situations.

These very different experiences increased my belief in the need for discernment and a genuine sense of calling to all forms of ministry. Every type of ministry contributes to the whole mission of the Church, and this diversity should be celebrated. Sadly, I have found that some priests display the opinion that parish ministry has a higher standing. Recently I spoke on separate occasions with two clergy concerned that their curates were struggling with parish life. Each said he thought his curate might be better off as a hospital chaplain, where pastoral weaknesses would not be exposed. Needless to say I strongly challenged their misguided assumptions about the nature of hospital ministry. I found it hurtful and disturbing to be confronted with such elitist attitudes, which left me with the impression that they viewed chaplaincy as a fallback job for those unable to cope with parish leadership. It would be helpful if post-ordination training positively promoted the equality and diversity of all forms of ordained ministry by inviting sector chaplains to speak about their distinctive ministries.

I was appointed to my present post of full-time coordinator of chaplaincy services six years ago. The department is responsible for providing spiritual care within a general acute hospital and a small local hospice. There is a considerable difference in the way spiritual care is offered within the two settings, especially with regard to the length of involvement that we have with the patients. This chapter focuses on my work within the hospital. It was my previous experience, as a hospital chaplain and as a housing manager, rather than any formal healthcare qualifications that led to my appointment. Healthcare chaplaincy is a specialized field within the NHS and I have built on my skills as part of continuing professional development. It does, however, concern me that experience can at times be viewed as secondary to academic qualifications. I lead a small multi-faith team of chaplains offering spiritual care to those of all faiths or none: to patients, their carers and staff. We meet this responsibility as fully as we are able, taking into consideration limited staffing levels – 2.45 whole-time equivalent. Importantly we are able to provide on-call cover, 24/7, for both the hospital and the hospice.

A significant part of my role involves managing the chaplaincy department. This includes responsibility for the budget, implementing policies and procedures, establishing audit tools, overseeing staff development and review and representing chaplaincy on several Trust committees, such as equality and diversity and end of life. Although this impacts significantly on my time, I am delighted that working in a small team means I can still have the privilege of directly delivering spiritual care.

As chaplains we routinely visit wards and departments. Our practice is never to take access to the wards for granted – we always seek permission from a senior nurse. Doing this builds up a relationship of trust with the staff, while allowing them to retain control of the care of the patients on their ward. Spiritual care is not fully understood by many members of staff, and most referrals we receive are for specific religious needs. We regularly offer training on this aspect of care to all levels of staff, part of which is to recognize the spiritual care they themselves offer through holistic care. Spiritual care at a basic level involves affirming each patient's uniqueness and creating opportunities for him or her to speak honestly about how illness has affected the whole self – body, mind and spirit. At all times it is the patient who retains control of what he or she wants to discuss, and we respect and affirm his or her spirituality. Unfortunately our contribution to the care of patients can go unrecognized. Because of the interpretation this hospital has of the 1998 Data Protection Act (DPA), we are not permitted to write in patients' notes.* As with all other employees, chaplains are bound by the Trust's strict confidentiality policy and we also conform to the healthcare chaplaincies' code of conduct. This extra level of national legislation seems unfair and detrimentally impacts on the care we offer.

I still gain most joy from the time I spend with patients and their relatives and carers. The hospital environment can be a strange and frightening place. From my own experiences as a patient it can be very easy to lose yourself amid numerous procedures that focus solely on treating the physical illness. The privilege of chaplaincy is to 'be with' rather than 'do to' the patient. Chaplains are an optional extra in that our involvement comes from being invited by the patient to enter his or her space. Whatever a patient's worldly status, for the time he or she is an inpatient the world shrinks to a bed, a chair and a locker. Some encounters might be viewed as mundane, the patient choosing to talk about everyday things such as the weather, television or sport. However, such conversations are important in providing an opportunity to reconnect with normality amid what could be a life-changing situation. Spending time with and actively listening to a patient is fundamental to offering spiritual care. I am always amazed how quickly some patients feel safe to speak about deep feelings and fears. In the parish situation building up relationships of trust takes time, but hospitalization and illness seem to lessen the need for such formalities.

It is an immense privilege to accompany people in times of extreme need but also stressful. I believe effective teamwork is vital, especially in providing mutual support to all chaplaincy members. Chaplains need to maintain their own spiritual well-being. It is only from strong secure self-knowledge and understanding that we can confidently work with those who are experiencing spiritual as well as physical pain. Often people ask me how I cope with the tragic situations I am involved in.

---

* Editors' note: guidance on the DPA issued by the Information Commissioner in April 2002 stated that sensitive personal data about patients can be processed without explicit consent where that processing is necessary for medical purposes. However, the guidance also took the view that the definition of medical purposes is not wide enough to include spiritual care. In relation to chaplains this ruling has been interpreted differently by different Trusts. Accordingly chaplaincy access to patient records varies greatly – within this book, for example, compare Joan's experience with that of Lance Blake (Chapter 12).

I honestly reply that if I only had myself to rely on I would fail miserably. Instead at such times I rely upon the grace of God to equip me. Having the support of friends and family is also very important.

Words cannot adequately describe the joy and sense of privilege I gain from ministering as a chaplain. The NHS and hospitals are constantly changing but whatever the future holds, I hope the specialist spiritual care chaplains offer to those of all faiths or none continues to be supported and valued as part of the holistic care afforded patients, relatives and staff.

12

The Rowans Hospice

LANCE BLAKE

When I look at a patch of dandelions I see weeds that are going to take over my garden. Children see flowers for Mum and little white parachutes you can free with a gentle puff.

The hospice offers a similar alternative view of our journey through life. A place of change, it is like a waterfall where the sleepy day-to-day flow of life is suddenly sent airborne over an unexpected ledge of painful truth. My role is as guide and companion to patients and their families during this journey. I also have the role of myth buster – no, hospice is not an elephant's graveyard where people go to die. Around half our patients return home with distressing symptoms alleviated and with greater resources to continue. Yes they will eventually die, but let us not forget that life itself is terminal.

As a novice Franciscan friar I was required to contemplate my own death. There is an irony in the fact that some patients only begin to live when they realize they are dying. Proximity to death clearly helps us decide what matters. I recall visiting a lady sitting tearfully on the edge of her bed. 'I've got everything you could want in life,' she said. 'We bought a new carpet last week – didn't need one, just fancied a change. It's standing in the corner of the lounge still in its cellophane wrapper, and today I've been told I have two weeks to live. I've just realized that all those things I thought important don't really matter.'

While the faithful of all belief systems may want to carry on with their rites and rituals, often in a hospice these become less important and sometimes a hindrance. It was a church commissioner who summoned me one morning. I had hardly entered her room when she blurted out, 'Lance, I'm **** scared.' I asked what she was struggling with and whether her faith gave her comfort. Her answer was a petrified 'no' as she admitted, 'All my life I've gone to church, said the prayers, administered my duties, but I've never formed a personal relationship with God. I feel lost and frightened.' We had about two weeks to begin to find her answers. I say 'we' and 'her' purposefully because, for our answers to be authentic and useful, we must own them.

Hospice chaplaincy has the advantage of being an integral part of a tightly knit multidisciplinary team. While hospital chaplains have struggled with the Data Protection Act, most hospices expect chaplains to write in patients' notes. Hospices have a broad understanding of spirituality: 'Spirituality is a quality that goes beyond religious affiliation, that strives for inspirations, reverence, awe, meaning and purpose, even in those who do not believe in God' (Murray and Zentner, 1989). This broad understanding is not going 'all secular' but recognizes that religion and faith can create problems. Spiritual care in a hospice is, therefore, not so much a case of opting in for a visit by the chaplain but more a case that you have to opt out. Even if patients opt out of a formal visit there is a good chance I will bump into them when they are on the way for a jacuzzi.

A South African gentleman I came to know through the 'jacuzzi run' personified this to perfection. His angry outbursts began to make sense as he acknowledged his own brutality having, during riots, bayoneted a pregnant woman. His pain was not the result of his cancer but the spiritual pain that engulfed him through the memory of his assault on another human. He see-sawed agonizingly between the God he refused and did not want to believe in and the God that he wanted but, by his own standards, would never accept him. Staying with him in this uncomfortable place eventually brought him to a resolution. Exhausted, he let go and let God love him.

In contrast, some spiritual pain comes more from what people have neglected to do or say. Fred confided one morning how he wished he had married Doris, his partner of 15 years. They had both been married before and, when their spouses died, had got together. Their partnership was their delight but in not cementing it formally it was now his pain. His relief was tangible when I told him that marriage was still possible. A civil service was followed by a blessing in the hospice chapel. Fred died two days later, calm, the restlessness gone.

Other uplifting experiences come with long overdue visits. Some of the best I have experienced have come when a 'black sheep' re-enters the sheepfold, a prodigal returns and the hospice facilitates healing and reconciliations. However, not all visits are rosy. More difficult to manage are those from lovers who, previously unknown to the family, suddenly surface to claim their part of a patient's life. Some realities and wounds go very deep, and supporting both sides requires confident juggling skills.

Another juggling contest arose with a Jewish patient. The kitchen was careful to get kosher food. However, when the chef asked Manny what he would like for breakfast, he replied, 'Pork sausages, please.' As in all religions there are degrees of adherence! However, the story continues.

The patient's son was very devout, phoning his rabbi regularly to ask what psalms to read and ritual to offer. Manny, though, did not want to be read to or fussed over. He just wanted his son to be there. Exploring whose needs were being met, and facilitating compromise, brought understanding and peace between them. In such 'go between' positions I am aware of 'the different roles within chaplaincy including that of pastor, minister, clown, counsellor and prophet' (Caring for the Spirit NHS Project, 2006).

Essentially, the chaplain's role is that of companion alongside the traveller in his or her journey. Even at journey's end there can still be some surprises. I vividly recall being at the side of a young man who had died, with his wife and six-year-old daughter present. The daughter asked me why there were two daddies in the room. At my request she elaborated, 'Well, I can see daddy lying on the bed but I can also see daddy standing by the door.' For a brief moment she could see into both dimensions of our being, and I explained what I thought this was about. Many people at the end of their life tell me they see loved ones who have already died – a quick check on the drug chart will usually confirm if it is a possible hallucination. This child, however, was not on medication. She saw what she saw, and my job was to help make sense of that.

Healing in hospice can be very different from hospital. Although death is the ultimate healing, we also help people to move towards wholeness, something perhaps more important than physical cure. Bishop Maurice Maddocks, when put on the spot about what healing meant to him, replied with the inspired quote, 'Christian healing is Jesus Christ meeting you at your point of need.' Chaplaincy shows its Christ-likeness in doing the same. It removes the sting of death and replaces it with a focus on life. As Dame Cicely Saunders (1976) wrote, 'We will do all we can not only to help you die peacefully, but also to live until you die.' Just before Cicely died, I asked her what qualities she would most look for in a hospice chaplain. She paused and then said, 'I would want someone who's been well battered by life.'

Maybe what makes hospice chaplaincy unique is its continual proximity to death. We are boundary people who occupy the 'departure lounge' between this world and the next. We daily witness changes at all levels from lively to lifeless, from wife to widow, from soulmate to single. Somewhere, within all this, we provide practical support while also weaving a theology of love and resurrection hope that holds the pain of change. When we get it right we know it completely. I will always remember June. Holding my hand as she died, she looked at me and said, 'I didn't realize that dying could be so beautiful.'

References

Caring for the Spirit NHS Project (2006), 'A Review of Some Theoretical Models of Healthcare Chaplaincy Service and Practice', available at <www.nhs-chaplaincy-collaboratives.com/resources/practicemodels0605.pdf> [accessed October 2010].

Murray, R. B. and Zentner, J. P. (1989), *Nursing Concepts for Health Promotion.* London: Prentice Hall.

Saunders, C. (1976), 'Care of the Dying: The Problem of Euthanasia'. *Nursing Times* 72/26, pp. 1049–52.

13

Sheffield Children's NHS Foundation Trust

BILL BURLEIGH

Sheffield Children's Hospital has a well-deserved reputation for skill and excellence in a range of paediatric disciplines. At around 150 beds, the hospital feels like the right size for a chaplain to get to know a lot of staff and become known to even more. However, the focus of almost all the work of the tiny chaplaincy department is with parents or with older children. Reaching out to the inner turmoil and dis-ease of parents is reaching out also to the child, even when tiny. This is because the peace and well-being of a parent often has an impact on the well-being and peace of the child.

In our hospital the three part-time chaplains only add up to one whole-time equivalent. This time-allocation includes our own management and secretarial tasks. Inevitably the team is rarely together. Handover notes are really important and, particularly following out-of-hours work, phone calls help the continuity of care. With the valuable support of our Muslim chaplain we try to visit every bedside. Parents usually stay with their child all day and sleep next to them at night. Some parents, who are with us for weeks or months, may be lucky enough to be allocated a bedroom in our overstretched parents' accommodation, resourced through a national charity. Unfortunately for most it is often a 24-hour vigil at the bedside.

Being a chaplain in a major children's hospital that is capable of amazing work for very seriously sick children brings both great joys and deep pain. There is joy in visiting the short-stay families, especially when they have heard the most longed-for words in the hospital, 'You can go home.' But there is deeper joy in the responses to the chaplains' offers of prayer. Recent analysis of our visiting records shows that after judging whether an offer of prayer would be right (that is, where there is anxiety and spiritual dis-ease), we offered to pray for or with 30 per cent of those we visited. On almost every occasion our offer was accepted. Only occasionally does a parent respond along the lines, 'Thanks, but that's not for me/us.' What is particularly heartening is that there is acceptance of offers of prayer by people across all faith groups *and* those where admission forms read 'religion: none'. For me the prayer that brings greatest joy is when the child leads or joins in with enthusiasm – that is precious.

But there is pain too, hurt that sometimes seems slowly to sap energy, even faith. To be with parents day by day or even month after month and then when, at the last, a long battle against the odds is finally lost, is a painful privilege. I remember flopping into a chair in the office of our intensive-care unit and expressing just how inadequate I felt alongside parents as the life of their child ebbed away. I hold as true wisdom the response of a consultant in that room, no doubt thinking of his task of breaking the worst of news to parents: 'It's not what you say that is remembered long afterwards but how you are – whether there is real compassion.'

The powerful strength of parents who have lost a child always amazes me. Here, surely, is the presence of God's power sustaining. The steady dignity I have seen over and over again on the faces of grief-stricken young parents at the funerals I am asked to lead restores my faith, as do the signs of deep supportive love as couples hold on to one another and, sometimes, to their other children too.

Many pains I feel as a chaplain are 'good' and indicate Christian empathy. However, there are other pains too of a very different nature, and these include frustration. I mean the frustration of feeling that one must battle through a secularist thread that runs through our hospital. 'Secularist' may be unfair in some instances; 'fear of failing to be politically correct' may be fairer. But both seem to manifest themselves in similar ways. Prayer, however broadly and sensitively composed, is resisted at hospital memorial services – this despite the clear majority of parents declaring some form of religious faith when asked at admission. I know that our part of the country has one of the lowest church attendance rates in the country but that in no way indicates – as our chaplaincy statistics show – any lack of spiritual awareness or wish for prayerful support.

Perhaps a more gentle pain or disappointment is illustrated by two incidents that happened one recent December. Christmas in the hospital begins with the switching-on of the lights festooned generously around the exterior of the buildings at the beginning of December. The event includes carols, a celebrity, hot chocolate and (still) the Christmas story. In the run-up to the event – not organized through the chaplaincy – I was asked if, this year, we could drop the story about Jesus since, 'It's not what children associate with Christmas any more.' The Gospel story stayed. The second event involved our wall-to-wall scene of Bethlehem in the chapel – hills, stars, villages and, in the corner, a stable with shredded-yellow-paper straw. Posters around the hospital invite anyone to visit the Bethlehem scene – 'Come to Bethlehem', 'How far is it to Bethlehem? Top floor in the chapel' and the like. How sad it is to walk along a corridor behind an eight-year-old child accompanied by a nurse who, pointing out a poster and asking, 'Have you been up to see Bethlehem?' gets the reply, 'Who is Bethlehem?' So next year and every year the scene will grow and new ways will be found to retell, with parents, the simple Christmas story.

Back to joys! And among these must rank the fact that we visit and support parents, children and staff of all faiths and none. Beyond the fairly limited sacramental ministry sought, our outreach is not denominationally defined. Sheffield is not yet a city with a great diversity of faiths, which may help us in our current minimal staffing. Together our spiritual support can reach to all.

If there are tensions for us as chaplains with our fellow clergy, they involve funerals. How important it is, we feel, to design every funeral we conduct around the family and the extent of their faith. Never have I found a lack of belief in a good afterlife for little ones (see Matthew 18.10). But how easy it is for clergy in parishes, who sometimes lead funerals we attend, to reach for 'the book' and cling to prayers and language that simply does not reach, indeed can anger, newly grieving parents. Why 'Merciful God ...' for a tiny infant? What on earth do 'vouchsafe', 'intercede' and the rest mean to young parents hanging on to a real, if informal, faith? Small wonder our local children's hospice is shy of clergy and turns to us. Huge flexibility is needed, it seems to me. Balloons, poems and 'fairy dust' may be wanted. That is fine, if leading to a gently worded prayer of commendation and freshly composed prayers for the aching family. How unfriendly so much in prayer books can seem; what a gap between traditional liturgical language and the lives of young 'unchurched' parents who have lost a child.

My conclusion? I would not swap this chaplaincy role for the world, even though it hurts so often. God's presence is clear to me in so many people, not because of miracles (though amazing things do happen) but because of love – and that's not the sole preserve of Christians or any other religious group.

14

Newcastle upon Tyne Hospitals NHS Foundation Trust

NIGEL GOODFELLOW

Two experiences from my first year in healthcare chaplaincy have stuck with me for the last 18 years. The first involves an amputee support group. As I entered the room Jim, the group's joker, said to the rest, 'Look out, here comes the chaplain. He's come to save our souls!' I am not sure how Jim expected me to react but my response, 'I'm a chaplain not a cobbler', was probably not the most tactful in a room full of amputees! However, it has been a useful anecdote and serves as a reminder of how careful we need to be with language; context can give even the simplest phrase an entirely different meaning from that intended. The second experience was an encounter with a doctor on an intensive-care unit who greeted me with, 'There's no one here for you today.' Puzzled, I returned to my senior colleague and discussed why she said this. We agreed that the only way to find out was to ask her. 'It's quite simple,' she said, 'there's no one dying here today.'

On the surface these two encounters are examples of 'ordinary' inter-actions between a chaplain and a patient or member of staff. But they are also classic examples of how the role can be stereotyped as to do with death and dying or narrowed to organized religion. Whether because much of our work is done confidentially and in the background or because chaplains have not been good at articulating what they do, such misconceptions are common. While healthcare chaplaincy has its roots in organized religion, its purpose is not to be a select ministry for a select group of people. My ministry involves the exercise of love, compassion and healing for all people irrespective of their background, race or creed. Such work is rooted in my particular belief system but I am not about making converts to that or any religious tradition. This can bring tensions when engaged in discussion with those who view ministry as about making converts to faith. Indeed it is not unusual for chaplains to be asked by some parish clergy, 'When are you going to come back and be a proper minister?'

What, though, does my ministry involve in practice? The workload can be split into four distinct categories. First, there are managerial and administrative tasks. It may seem strange that I begin with this but I currently head a department that serves a large teaching hospital with 2,000 beds and over 11,000 staff spread across five sites. The chaplaincy team consists of 8 full- and part-time staff plus over 80 volunteers. Chaplaincy is not immune from the issues that affect service delivery in the modern NHS. Consequently I am expected to ensure that the department is run in line with corporate-governance and human-resource policies. Similarly we must deliver a service that is value for money and effective in meeting the overall aims of the Trust. My responsibilities include the department's budget; appointing and managing the chaplaincy team, including staff appraisal and development, sickness and disciplinary management; recording and monitoring chaplaincy activity; managing the department's strategy and service development; and liaising with local and faith communities to ensure their engagement and participation in the life of the hospital and the chaplaincy department.

I am also involved in supporting the corporate management team as they develop the Trust's bereavement policy, religious and spiritual-care policy, equality and diversity work and staff support and well-being work. As chaplains we have significant contact with patients, staff and the local community. Accordingly our involvement with managerial, administrative and policy development allows the wider managerial team of the hospital to remain in contact with the consequences of their work in a very real way.

Second, there is pastoral care of patients, relatives, visitors and staff. Being in hospital can be a very disorientating experience. Despite all best efforts the environment is often alien and sometimes very frightening. Personal space and information has to be shared. While preserving privacy and self-respect is a key concern, many patients still feel their dignity to be compromised. Being a supraregional centre, patients are frequently referred to us from vast distances for specialist care, so finding themselves miles from home and normal support systems. Within such a melting pot of experience, thoughts about the meaning of life, family concerns and worries over coping tend to emerge. Left unaddressed these concerns can have a huge effect on the way people cope with what is happening to them. As chaplains we are employed as part of the multidisciplinary team to be there for people as they try to make sense of what is happening to them or their loved ones. Sharing people's journeys through dis-ease or uncertainty, we enable them to find their own ways of living life to the full. This support may take various forms. Most obviously, we make space for people to talk about what is happening to them in a safe, independent and confidential way. Sometimes this will extend to being an advocate for patients who find themselves in conflict with their families or clinical-care team. Following a death we may be involved with providing practical and emotional support to the bereaved. This can include accompanying them to the mortuary viewing facilities.

The NHS is an organization constantly undergoing change. New procedures and new ways of working are facts of life – the boundaries of what can clinically be done are being pushed on an almost daily basis. From ethical dilemmas to management demands, staff are not immune from the pressures that working in such an environment brings. Our work with staff includes advocacy when they find themselves under pressure or facing disciplinary measures. On a routine basis we also provide formal and informal support and debrief following critical incidents.

Third, there is religious care. For some patients, relatives, visitors and staff, religion continues to be an important part of their lives. While the role of the chaplain is broader than the religious, we are still responsible for ensuring that religious needs are met. Acting as a bridge between the hospital and local faith communities, we ensure that the specific needs of each community can be met to the best of the hospital's abilities. Examples of our work in this area include maintaining a directory of contacts with faith communities for staff to access, as well as organizing education events for staff to dialogue with faith-community representatives. We also provide information to staff about each faith community in our locality so that they have information on how patients' beliefs might impact on their care – rituals around birth and death, dietary requirements and so on. This information quite literally runs from A (atheist) to Z (Zoroastrian).

We organize acts of worship and times of reflections around traditional faith events or important moments in the life of the hospital, and also conduct rites of passage such as baptisms, weddings and acts of remembrance. In 2009/10 the chaplaincy team had contact with about 4,000 people through Sunday worship and 92 families who wished to mark their child's birth with a religious ceremony. We also conducted over 120 funerals, for which the hospital had a legal responsibility, and ministered to nearly 2,000 people who attended annual memorial services arranged for maternity, paediatrics and critical-care units in the hospital. In many cases religious care is requested or worship attended by people who do not have an active faith background. This presents the chaplain with the task of making links between faith and life in a way that sometimes transcends traditional boundaries. This is both exciting and at times challenging.

Fourth and finally, there is education and research. Working in a teaching hospital brings with it a responsibility to ensure that there is an engagement with the continuing development of healthcare and its provision. The chaplaincy team is, therefore, committed to the training and development programme of the Trust. We have links with universities and external organizations involved in research and development in religious and spiritual care, ethics and chaplaincy studies. The department is also actively engaged in teaching programmes for all levels of staff in areas such as end-of-life care, bereavement, listening skills, ethics and equality and diversity.

15

Rotherham, Doncaster and South Humber Mental Health NHS Foundation Trust

CHARLES THODY

My first foray into the world of mental-health chaplaincy was when I fell ill while I was a parish priest. Something quite horrendous had happened within my extended family, and the pressure of trying to deal with it all eventually became too much. Feeling the pressure, I had attempted to speak to a GP some months before but was simply told, 'Go home, listen to some classical music and remember we all have pressured lives.' This was a far from helpful response, rather like saying, 'Pull yourself together' – something that should never be said to a person with any form of mental illness. As a result I feared approaching the GP until the inevitable happened some months later and I cracked. Now I really did need help. This time I saw a different GP, who simply said, 'You are here, you have admitted to the pressure, you are over the worst. Now tell me about it.' I could have hugged her. Without entering into detail, I was signed off work with reactive depression. It was Ash Wednesday.

Two days later, still battling with what had happened to me, feeling lonely and wondering what to do next, there came a knock on the door. A senior member of the clergy stood there, a person whom I had feared (yet respected) for some time. Instead of the challenge that I expected came the words, 'Now, where's the kettle? Let's see what I can do for you.' In our ensuing discussion I found that this person had been, for many years, a mental-health chaplain. He was the only person, apart from the second GP, who had spoken to or treated me as a human being and not as some kind of outcast.

After a period of rest I returned to work. Four years later I was exploring what the future might hold. In conversation with my mentor of the time, I was asked, 'Why don't you consider this mental-health post? It's new and I think you might like it.' My instant and instinctive reaction was to laugh. I had no training in mental healthcare. I was an aircraft-design engineer who had entered ministry later in life. 'But you are human, you've had some personal insight, and we can offer you any practical training you need – please, at least go and look at the job.'

I did, and ten years on I find myself the head of chaplaincy of a large mental-health trust that covers a huge area – units span from as far west as Manchester to as far east as Grimsby. In between I developed and managed a chaplaincy service for men with dangerous and severe personality disorders, and a multi-faith team in a high-security forensic hospital, with all the challenges and changes that brought. I often look back over the past ten years and wonder how I got here, and conclude that God has a sense of humour!

So what have I learnt about chaplaincy? Some would have us believe that to be a chaplain in the modern NHS we must be able to jump through certain hoops, abide by certain codes and collect so many points, as 'points make prizes'. I am sceptical. I am a great believer in being professional in all that we do, in becoming incarnate within the places that we serve, in offering a service that our fellow healthcare professionals respect and embrace; yet, above all, I am a great believer in being human.

That perhaps sounds obvious coming from a priest. Yet I do live in fear that the 'humanness' of chaplaincy is in danger of being swallowed up in the bureaucracy of an ever changing and challenging NHS. Mental wellness is all about our humanity, about how we relate to ourselves and others, about how (as individuals and as communities) we function within the world around us. This is a constant challenge and paradox when, as a manager, I am also having to deal with targets, budgets and the latest innovations from above, such as the Knowledge and Skills Framework. It always fascinates me how, whenever there is a change in the structure of the NHS or a new innovation, the 'system' is never too sure where or how the chaplains fit. We don't always sit comfortably in the hierarchy, and long may that continue.

But then I look at the Judaeo-Christian tradition from which I come and I see Jesus in a similar position. Here was a man who did not fit comfortably into the 'system' and was not frightened of challenging it. Part of his humanity was to enter into the world of the unfamiliar, the world of others outside the system. He touched the lepers, ate with the outcasts, sat with the 'unclean' and challenged the society around him. He lived a paradox that made other people feel, at times, extremely uncomfortable.

One of the greatest joys for me in past years was my work within a multi-faith team of chaplains. I recall the difficulty in drawing this together, in – for example – convincing the system that a Pagan chaplain was just as important as a Christian one. I found great depths in my own faith and spirituality that I never knew existed when, on many occasions, I sat with chaplains of other faiths as they offered care and support to disturbed patients. I shall never forget the day when about 12 of us sat together and debated and discussed our differences and similarities – nor the look on my line manager's face when a Roman Catholic bishop and a Pagan Wiccan chaplain sat together and debated not only their own beliefs but those of a patient they had both met and worked with. My line manager never forgot that day either; it was a turning point where she saw chaplaincy at its best.

Two particular stories inspire me as a mental-health chaplain. The first is the Gerasene demoniac (Mark 5.1–20 and Luke 8.26–39). There is no room here to discuss the story at length, but it provides a model of mental-health chaplaincy. Where all others show fear and disdain to the demoniac, Jesus simply asks, 'What is your name?' He connects immediately with the humanity in the tormented man. I once read this story to a group of patients diagnosed with paranoid schizophrenia and they all, without prompting or having heard the story before, recognized themselves in it. At the heart of care for them were not the drugs or the 'talking therapies' but the recognition of their human nature behind their condition. It was an amazing moment.

The second relates to St Aidan of Lindisfarne. Legend has it that he walked from kingdom to kingdom, learning the context in which people lived and the language they spoke, not judging them by their actions or beliefs but loving them for who they were and helping them to recognize something of the divine within themselves. This to me is the role of the mental-health chaplain.

As we travel through life we touch other people's lives and they ours at different levels. We are in danger, in institutions, of becoming institutionalized. If that happens we lose contact with each other's humanity. The paradox of mental-health chaplaincy for me is the tension of holding together the needs of the institution with the needs of the people it serves; learning the language of both and learning to love both. As a chaplain and a manager I sometimes have to walk a scary and wobbly tightrope between the two. Being a chaplain in the modern NHS is a challenging place to be. No longer is it simply the old model of the Church in the hospital. The modern mental-health chaplain must be prepared to walk that tightrope and even at times be the clown.

Part 4

CHAPLAINS' STORIES –
THE PRISON SERVICE

16

HMP Wandsworth

TIM BRYAN

Unequivocally, being a chaplain has been the most exciting and fulfilling role I have ever had. Ordained as a minister in secular employment, I continued as a detective inspector until called to full-time prison ministry in 2006. There are days when I go into prison soon after 7.30 a.m. and emerge, 13 hours later, with a sense of complete absorption by the events and people I have been caught up with. Not that all is marvellous – far from it – but there are precious spiritual moments when you become aware of God's being involved in someone's life or the daily events of the prison in a real, transforming and powerful way.

Entering Wandsworth can be daunting. This is the largest prison in the country. The dense Victorian site, filled with gates and locks, is not a place for the fragile or claustrophobic. This is an enclosed community, shielded from view by high brick walls topped with razor wire, with approximately 1,650 prisoners and 750 staff of varying colour, ethnicity, religion and sexuality. An international environment, Wandsworth reflects the diversity of London and those passing through the criminal justice system. In addition to ethnic and religious diversity there are also different categories of prisoners: sentenced prisoners whose terms vary from literally a few days to life; remanded prisoners awaiting trial or sentencing; and detained prisoners held under immigration legislation. The prison has two separate units: the smaller, originally built as a women's prison, is used as a vulnerable persons' unit for men who risk being assaulted if located in the main prison. These comprise primarily convicted sex offenders but also others who have threats of serious violence against them. In the prison as a whole many prisoners have enduring complex mental-health needs or struggle with addictions or other anti-social tendencies. This makes them restless and at times challenging to manage. There is constant potential for serious incidents of violence or self-harm, day and night.

Most days there will be some form of religious service or activity prepared by a chaplain. In addition to the Christian tradition, the Prison Service offers access to the other major world faiths. There are valuable spaces for worship, including a church, a mosque and a multi-faith area used by Sikhs, Hindus, Buddhists, Jews and Christians. It is interesting to note that the vast majority of chaplaincy visitors and volunteers are Christian, reflecting the clear gospel imperative of Matthew 25.35–36.

For me ministry within the prison is rooted in this imperative and shaped by the Anglican understanding of the cure of souls. It is an inclusive ministry, not seeking to convert but confident in the call to serve and bear witness to a God of love, mercy and justice. Through Bible studies, Prison Alpha, fellowship, prayer, worship and testimony of churches, we have witnessed God moving powerfully among his people, changing attitudes, softening hearts and bringing people to faith.

Part of the chaplaincy's ministry is to the wider Church and, increasingly, to other faith communities. This takes a number of approaches: encouraging faith leaders to support men sent to prison with sustained contact and fellowship; challenging faith communities to see what prison and prisoners are about and whether they have the vision and capacity to offer ongoing support and discipleship to ex-offenders on release. I oversee a broad range of world-faith chaplains – Sikh, Hindu, Buddhist, Jewish, Muslim and Pagan. While such faiths have a clear involvement within the prison, for some this external engagement is still embryonic.

No member of the chaplaincy team, paid or voluntary, is allowed to proselytize. This helpfully protects us from those of various faiths and denominations who would see prison as a recruiting ground. However, this in no way restricts our ability to listen to the genuine concerns people have about meaning, unresolved guilt and anger, and often a desire to connect to something they have known from childhood as God. The effect of prison is sometimes to confront people with something about themselves that they have been running away from: a relationship, a destructive behaviour, an addiction. Frequently the desire and willingness to confront these things is associated with the greater structure and constraint that prison provides, and some form of spiritual awakening. As Alexander Solzhenitsyn (2002) so eloquently put it, 'Bless you prison . . . For there . . . I came to realize that the object of life is . . . the maturity of the human soul.'

On an average weekday over 30 new prisoners can arrive at Wandsworth. Given the varied emotional responses to coming into prison, the chaplain's day begins with visits to each of the new 'receptions' to welcome and offer practical, emotional and spiritual support. We bring information about the multi-faith chaplaincy services. As well as the world-faith chaplains noted above, there is also a range of Christian denominations. Accordingly we are able to accommodate most religious traditions. Initial responses are further complicated when English is not the first language.

Sometimes we are able to assist with practical things like letting families know people are here and how to visit. Sometimes our role is just to listen and offer reassurance. Before leaving we record a person's religious tradition and whether there is a wish to attend the relevant faith community services. We also report any concerns about mental state or any indication that the prisoner has a previous history of self-harm or mental illness.

Following the morning senior managers' meeting chaired by the No. 1 Governor, a meeting that offers real opportunity for chaplaincy to understand and occasionally affect how things are done, we start a round of pastoral activities. This includes seeing prisoners in specialist units (such as healthcare or the separation unit), participating in multi-disciplinary reviews of prisoners considered at risk of self-harm or suicide, and responding to the myriad requests for assistance from prisoners. While some requests are specifically faith-based, the majority require more general care. Operating within the constraints of prison rules, chaplains must learn or develop effective pastoral-care skills. This is essential for the team to be seen not as a bunch of mavericks but as people concerned with decency and fairness, who advocate on behalf of others, be they prisoners, their families or staff.

Life in all its rawness has the potential to overwhelm the image of God. It is difficult for some to imagine ministering to prisoners. For me the challenge has been less about the environment. Having spent a career in the police there was very much a sense of the Lord preparing me for the rawer aspects of prison life. The greater challenge is in the working out of my ministry to prisoners and staff alike. I have observed both contrast and commonality in the experience of all those who live and work in the prison and continually grapple with how best to minister effectively and relevantly.

Sadly Wandsworth has experienced a number of prisoner deaths recently. Whatever the cause, all involve chaplains offering direct support to cellmates and friends, family members and staff. It is a difficult and sometimes protracted time and casts a cloud over the prison. This is a specific example of when the pastoral skills of the chaplain are appreciated. As in other settings, there is no easy way to approach bereavement. My experience is that people appreciate direct and clear information and space to respond and be heard.

Sometimes it is possible to see the work of God in someone's life over a period of years – authentic spiritual roots put down and attitudes and behaviour changed. One such man has worked for the chaplaincy team as our orderly for a year. Serving a considerable sentence for robbery, he is able to speak personally of the Lord's renewal and restoration. There are also extraordinary sorrows: a member of staff commits suicide, people experience marital break-up, life-changing accidents occur, a loved one dies. All strike at the heart of people and communities and remind us of our frailty and search for meaning. There are no easy answers, just a journeying with people in their pain and confusion.

If you read a job description for a chaplain you will see listed the religious requirements and competencies. Obviously there is a need to fulfil the faith requirements and a personal antecedent history that satisfies the various vetting procedures, including counter-terrorism checks. Even for a volunteer, prison chaplaincy is physically and emotionally demanding. You need to be fit in every sense of the word. However, the qualities most desired are wisdom, compassion and humility; rounded off with a robust sense of humour.

Reference

Solzhenitsyn, A. (2002), *The Gulag Archipelago: 1918–1956*. New York: Perennial Classics.

17

HMP Wakefield

DAWN COLLEY

As I was presenting a poster of my research a woman approached. I thought, 'Great, someone who is going to show interest in my project on self-harm.' However, her question was, 'So do you sit and talk with men who you know are rapists and murderers? Are you not afraid?' My response to this question is twofold. First, that at least I know who I am dealing with, alarm buttons are close at hand and trained officers close by; to a certain degree this is safer than encountering strangers in a café. Second, that the day I forget the capacity of the people I work with, and their victims, is the day I should cease being a chaplain. Complacency is not an option in a high-security prison.

As a chaplain you get to understand what Jesus faced as he associated with 'sinners and tax collectors'. I am never sure how a prospective employer would respond to the phrase, 'She regularly associates with murderers and rapists. She appears able to cross boundaries and work with people at all levels.' This may look like a poor statement to have on your CV but as a statement for the values of the Kingdom it goes a long way.

Chaplains work for the Ministry of Justice. Under the surface there is always the question: 'How does criminal justice compare with God's justice?' Currently, within government policy, there is a focus on restorative justice. The aim is to enable victims to feel restoration has been sought, that injustice has not gone unmarked, but also that this punishment does not remain a continuous barrier. This clearly echoes several biblical examples of judgement and restoration. In Genesis 4.10–15 Cain is excluded from the community but also protected so that no others may harm him. In Mark 5.1–20 Jesus removes the demons from the man called Legion. However, the challenge was for the man to return to the community he had harmed and prove that he was changed, and for the community to accept him. This is the role of the chaplain: to represent God to each individual, to meet people where they are and to witness to God's love.

Faith is recognized as an important part of a person's moral compass, and for this reason chaplains of all faiths are called to support prisoners.

As a chaplain you need to be respectful of other faiths, facilitating fitting services. Organizing and running groups for a range of denominations and faiths calls for openness to doing things differently and the furthering of ecumenical and multi-faith dialogue. Due to the proportion of prisoners still registering as nominally Christian, it remains the case that a majority of chaplains are Christian. It is frustrating that multi-faith working can be easier than Christian ecumenism.

Working within a prison brings the joys and sorrows of church ministry within a wall. Walking alongside prisoners in times of trouble, grief and distress is central to the role. Daily visits to prisoners in isolation or at the healthcare unit represent outreach to the outcast and ill. Chaplains are key people in informing prisoners of illness or death within their families. Similarly, when there is a death in custody, chaplains help support the community and work alongside the family liaison officer informing the next of kin. In such cases there is always a coroner's hearing, and chaplains are often invited to attend and support both the officers involved and any family present.

Subsequent to a prisoner's death, chaplains are sometimes asked to participate in the funeral. Alongside this it is recognized that the prison community is grieving, and a memorial service may be organized. This has to be done sensitively as those who attend may be of different faiths or none. Likewise, in the event of an officer's death the community grieves and needs supporting. Even where chaplains are not asked to organize such services there is the expectation that they should be present to offer support to the whole community.

Over recent years an increasing emphasis on human rights has created a vast swing in the way that discipline is enforced within a prison. To some staff it occasionally appears that prisoners have more rights than those working to protect the public. The principle is that prisoners should have the same access to medical treatment, religious freedom and education that is available outside. Sometimes these aspects appear to be better inside. Prisoners are excused from work in order to attend worship, for example, but staff by contrast are expected to follow shift patterns that may prevent them attending theirs. Similarly I have heard staff complain that while sick and at-risk prisoners are allocated a constant watch officer to ensure their well-being, their own elderly parents struggle to access services. On these occasions the role of the chaplain is to listen and to support.

On the other hand, following the death of a relative, prisoners are sometimes unable to spend time with family or attend the funeral. It is not uncommon to hear from discipline staff, 'Well they should have thought about that when they were committing their crime.' At these times the chaplain is called to remind staff of the humanity in all people – regardless of their acts – and ensure that the prisoners are offered alternative support.

As a chaplain it is important to note that you are employed as 'prison' chaplain, not as 'prisoner' chaplain. Getting the balance right between walking alongside prisoners, officers and governors is imperative: if you are too friendly with prisoners the officers will not open up to you; if you are too friendly with the officers the prisoners will not trust you; if you are too friendly with the governors no one will speak with you! In this place of hierarchy, power and authority a chaplain is called to represent God to all. This involves crossing boundaries, seeing all perspectives, praying for the institution, challenging at all levels when this is right and, ultimately, using insight and wisdom to strive for God's justice to be done.

In the current climate of budget cuts the role of the chaplain has come under scrutiny. What is it that chaplains do that a social worker could not? Would it not be cheaper to get local faith leaders to lead the acts of corporate worship? Thankfully the Prison Service has recognized that chaplains are not just isolated to faith-specific work but play a crucial role in the whole of the prison. Chaplaincy, for example, brings in support from the community, from volunteers helping to run groups to churches leading fellowship and expressing the hope that restoration and support are available beyond the walls.

As that suggests, chaplains play a crucial role in bridging the gap between prison and the world outside. Talks given at churches, schools and so on all play a part in raising concepts of justice and forgiveness in society. One thing that never ceases to amaze me is the outrage of the press and public in the event of suicide within prison, alongside the attitude towards some that, 'We would kill them if they ever got out.' Sadly, especially with paedophiles, society often shows an unwillingness to believe in restoration or to show trust in the criminal justice system.

Being a chaplain is a constant challenge. Every day you are faced with an incredible range of situations: the depravity of humanity, the hope of something better, the call for justice, the challenge of ecumenical, multi-faith and multi-disciplinary working, walking the tightrope of representing God to all people. This comes with a hazard warning: there will be moments of darkness and despair when individuals progress and then return to offending, when the institution marginalizes the role of faith, when the balance between pastoral care and security/trust issues becomes skewed. At such times it is important to have a strong prayer life and the humility and integrity to access support through supervision within the Prison Service and spiritual direction.

In a prison you are called to search for the godliness in people whom society has banished for doing ungodly deeds. You are called to bring light to a place of darkness, to bring joy to places of despair. Ultimately you are called to hold to the central premise of the gospel that, regardless of who you are or what you have done, God can save. 'Then he said, "Jesus, remember me when you come into your kingdom." He replied, "Truly I tell you, today you will be with me in Paradise"' (Luke 23.42–43).

18

HMP Low Newton

DANA DELAP

HMP Low Newton is a closed, female prison and young-offender institution, serving a region from the Scottish Borders to north Yorkshire and north Cumbria. It holds just over 300 prisoners serving sentences from a few days to life, plus those on remand. There are a small number of juveniles and a wing for prisoners with dangerous and severe personality disorders.

The first thing I do in the morning is read the journal. Since most of the chaplains are part-time we rely on the journal as our main source of communication. Each encounter with a prisoner, every worship service, group and meeting are written in the journal. In the course of any day chaplains will meet women who have asked for pastoral support, who need to talk, to light a candle after bereavement or to make their confession. Chaplains will plan and lead services, discipleship courses and seekers groups. They will make statutory visits to the sick and new prisoners, attend meetings, write reports and be available for prisoners and staff in crisis. The journal encapsulates the life of the prison community, its 'going out and coming in'.

The journal also forms the basis of our prayers. These reflect the story the journal tells of people who met chaplains the day before. The chaplaincy 'welcome leaflet' promises to pray each day for the prison, inmates and staff. Occasionally I am held to account. 'Have you prayed for me today?' a woman might ask as I leave the chapel to walk down to the wings.

It is part of our statutory duties to visit new prisoners within 24 hours of their arrival. Women make up about 5 per cent of the total prison population but often have more complex needs. Most women suffer significant loss through their imprisonment. They might lose their jobs, their homes, their partners, even their children. It is estimated that some 18,000 children in England and Wales have mothers in prison. If no family carer can be found they may be freed for adoption without consent. Between 70 and 80 per cent of the women are withdrawing from addictive substances. It can take two weeks of detoxification before new receptions are sufficiently released from addiction to be coherent, and months before the craving stops. New prison receptions bring a plethora of domestic and personal chaos, so listening to their stories may take most of the morning.

Then I visit prisoners who are in the healthcare unit and those who are segregated in the care and separation unit. Around 80 per cent of women prisoners have mental-health problems. Because of the failures of 'Care in the Community', people with mental-health problems can fall through the net of social care. Speaking on *Law in Action* in 2007, Anne Owers, Chief Inspector of Prisons, described prisons as 'care in custody'. Chaplains visit the healthcare unit daily and get to know well the prisoners held there. They share with us letters from home, hopes for release and dreams for the future.

Women often ask me for prayer. Sometimes I pray there and then, in a cell, on the corridor, in a workshop or classroom. Prison is the only place I have knelt to pray with a stranger on the floor beside a bed. It is a privilege to be with someone who wants to open her heart to God. The women usually ask for prayer for friends, children and families, and a request for prayer usually leads to further meetings and the chance to listen to their stories. These can be shocking and sometimes I am moved to tears.

More than half of all women prisoners have been victims of abuse, whether in childhood or as adults. Chaplains work with other staff to build up self-esteem through encouragement, affirmation and challenge. Vulnerable prisoners are at risk of suicide and self-harm – in all my encounters I am vigilant to that. Keeping women safe is a priority, especially when they have received bad news. The prison relies on chaplains to tell women that a relative or friend has died. To hear that someone you love has died is always terrible, especially if you are unable to attend the funeral; to be unable to be with others who loved that person brings a particular pain of separation and loss. Sometimes the women have mixed emotions about the death, involving guilt or relief as well as sadness. I do not have answers but find time to sit and keep vigil with the bereaved.

My favourite part of the day is dinnertime, when the corridors are crowded with women returning from work. If I have time I lean against the radiator near the chapel and wait to see who will stop and talk to me. It might be someone who comes to chapel regularly, someone I do not know who wants to talk or a member of staff who needs to offload. For me this is incarnational ministry at its most poignant.

In the afternoon I lead a group on the wing for those serving life sentences. Some are Christians, one is Pagan, others would describe themselves as non-religious. We are all on a journey. I have found that most women pray at some point during arrest, conviction and imprisonment.

Offering practical support in developing spirituality is key to discipleship. As the women learn to express themselves, find a voice to speak to and of God, they gradually engage in more traditional forms of faith development such as Prison Alpha.

In my group of life-sentence prisoners the women want to know why I am leaving to become an ordinand. They thought I was a priest anyway. I explain that I want to be able to feed them with Holy Communion. That makes more sense to them. For many, Holy Communion is a high point in the week when they feel a sense of belonging to the church community both within and outside the walls. They like the idea of my being able to baptize those who come to faith. One asks if I will come back and baptize her. I tell them, sadly, that I need to go away to train and that it will take some years. I will miss the prisoners very much but promise to keep on praying for them, and they offer to reciprocate.

The role of prison is to protect the public and reduce reoffending. For me the role of chaplains is to recognize that prisoners can be both sinners and saints and to offer the hope of transformation. I love listening to the life stories of the women. They may be speaking for the first time about what they have done and what has happened to them. Searching for the golden threads of God's presence in their journeys, they begin to understand that sin has brought them to a moment when they are in prison, but God's love can bring change and hope for the future.

Chaplains are not only there as agents of individual change. Prisons are designed for men, by men. For women prison is often a disproportional response to offending. However, until social circumstances are addressed there is little alternative. Poverty, poor education, unemployment and inability to gain access to social services all contribute to social exclusion. Nearly 30 per cent of women in prison are black or minority ethnic – there is a race as well as gender bias in the criminal justice system. Chaplains are advocates for those who find it hard to give voice to their needs, and some form active links between the prisoners and the community.

The advantage of a diverse team is that we share roles. The coordinating chaplain manages a team that may include full-time, part-time and sessional chaplains and all recognized faiths. We rarely worship together but can share silence and celebrations. In our prison the Roman Catholic Mass is held on Saturday and the other Christian chaplains share Sunday services. Preaching in the prison has spoilt me. In my parish I am always disappointed that people do not interact with me – I have got used to being interrupted and challenged. Jesus spoke in John 5 of doing what he saw the Father already involved with. I see my job as looking out for signs of God working in people's lives and blessing that.

At the end of the day I write up the journal detailing the journey of the prison community during this day. Tomorrow, other chaplains will be accompanying the prisoners and staff; praying, supporting, challenging, loving and most of all listening to the voices of those whose stories the Church usually excludes.

Reference

Law in Action (2007), BBC Radio 4, 25 September.

19

HMPs Acklington and Castington

CHRIS HUGHES

Located about 30 miles north of Newcastle and 4 miles west of the small fishing port of Amble, these are the most northern prison establishments in England. The two low-level security category 'C' prisons share a former RAF site in a sparsely populated part of the country where moorland merges with farmland. Wherever prisons are situated, those in them can be perceived as on the margins of society. For those imprisoned at Acklington and Castington the geographical extremity of this site, especially for family and friends dependent on public transport, reinforces this sense of being on the edge.

It was to this edge, of society and country, that I was asked to work about nine hours a week as a sessional Roman Catholic chaplain. I have not been in post long so these are the initial reflections of one learning about the context and role. The remainder of my work is as a priest in the ex-mining town of Bedlington and its neighbouring villages, 15 miles south of the prisons. Working on a very part-time basis, with the majority of my time in the parish, I sense that my prisons ministry is on 'the edge of an edge'.

This reflection is in two parts. The first is on how prison chaplaincy can be a living sign and instrument of mediation and redemption on the edge of prison life. The second acknowledges some dimensions of my being on the edge of this edge.

Prisons are places where legitimate values clash. Our society primarily upholds the dignity of the human person by ensuring that the freedom of the individual is cherished and protected. However, the value of the state in being able to protect people from harm and punish people to ensure that crimes are not repeated is also seen as a legitimate value. Despite debates concerning the effectiveness of sentencing policies, few people would wish to deny the state the right to take away the liberty of others under certain strict conditions. The freedom of the individual and the right of the state to protect and punish are not the only values that collide. Society allows for religious liberty and plurality, which has often meant that religious perspectives, though valued, are marginalized as 'private'. When asked about the significance of faith for a recent UK government, its then director of communications infamously declared, 'We don't do God.' Yet within the prison system, an institution that is an agent of the secular state, we see religious perspectives integrated into the management and operational structures. Chaplains have statutory duties to see new arrivals, those in sick bays and those in segregated cells.

It is within this space where values clash that prison chaplaincy appears to 'live and move and have its being'. Ensuring that the prison system does what it needs to do, without infringing on any more rights of the human person than necessary, is a task of prison chaplaincy. Since freedom is so crucial to the dignity of the human person, chaplaincy in the prisons I work in has a role to ensure that when freedom is denied, the dignity of the person is perceived and upheld, including by the inmate himself. Representing a religious perspective and supporting religious freedom within a secular institutional mindset is another role for chaplaincy. Here I see Gillian Rose's idea of the 'broken middle' (Shanks, 2008) as being highly significant for understanding prison chaplaincy. In these tasks chaplaincy has a mediating role, seeking to integrate the different perspectives and values to ensure that none of them is wholly dominated by the other.

During these early experiences I have often been reminded of a statement made by Sr Helen Prejean (self-described 'death-penalty nun' famously portrayed in the film *Dead Man Walking*). At a talk in Newcastle in 2008 she said, and I paraphrase, 'If redemption means anything, it means that we are not to define a person by the worst thing they have done.' In the prison context a person is defined by the worst thing they have done (or been found out doing). Yet in my engagement with prisoners it is clear that the dynamic of redemption does operate – these people are clearly more than the worst thing they have done. Sin operates but so does grace! Prison chaplaincy has the potential and calling to embody and celebrate this truth of redemption.

One of the interesting dynamics of there being fewer Roman Catholic priests in this country has been an increase in lay people in official roles of ministry. This is especially the case in chaplaincy. Within my own diocese the majority of chaplains in healthcare, education and prison contexts are not ordained priests. Perhaps more interestingly, especially in the context of Roman Catholic ministry, the vast majority of lay chaplains are women. Priests do have a role but this is to carry out those tasks a lay person cannot. Accordingly I have one major task as a sessional chaplain and that is to preside at three Eucharists during the week. While I do feel a bit of a 'mass machine', I do not wish to play down the significance of this, nor forget that significant relationships are created with those attending the Eucharists. But it does mean my role is limited. I sense that some important theological questions need to be asked as to where lay chaplains get their authority and what this means for a Roman Catholic understanding of ministry in general. This is not an attempt to undermine lay chaplaincy or ministry. Having heard stories of how some lay chaplains have found it difficult to work with clergy and how for many clergy it is rare to work with the lay chaplain who has the senior role, it is important that some attempt be made to outline the theological significance of the role of the lay chaplain. This is necessary so that a lay chaplain can have the confidence and authority to operate in such situations. There is also the question concerning the nature of the ministry of the part-time priest who has a limited role of celebrating sacraments. It is important that my role be not just as a sacramental dispenser but that the celebration of the sacraments connects to and links with the healing, reconciling, witnessing and bearing of hope and compassion that is carried by all the chaplaincy team.

Although my chaplaincy role is limited, one strength of having two roles is that there is great potential for these two areas of ministry, prison and parish, to feed mutually from each other. For example, celebrating the Eucharist with a small group means that I can experiment with sermons. At Pentecost I did an 'Examen' exercise with the prisoners based on the 'fruit of the Spirit' passage (Galatians 5.22–23). Since it went well it gave me confidence to try it with the parish. Equally, my time in the prison can be a source of inspiration that feeds my parish ministry. While respecting confidentiality I can share with the parish profound stories and experiences encountered from my chaplaincy, and I hope that my experience in that role can help reconfigure the pre-conceptions and prejudices about prisons and prisoners that arise from some areas of the media. I can also see potential for parishioners to be a resource for prison chaplaincy work. Local parishioners do volunteer in the prison but the scope of work carried out could be greater. This mutual interaction between parish and prison ministries is at a formative stage but I sense that development in this area is possible.

The gardens at the two prisons are beautiful. On fine spring and summer days the grace and beauty of nature – blue skies, wonder-proclaiming flowers, the swooping, soaring and song of birds – stand in strong contrast to the brutish imposition on the Northumbrian landscape of ugly concrete walls, high gates and the weaving of barbed wire throughout. This stark contrast is, for me, a symbol of the human reality within the prison system. The ugliness of the damage of the prisoners' crimes, and the damage that has been done to them either individually or systemically, leave their mark. But this coexists with the beauty and hope of humanity created in the image and likeness of

God and called to share in the fullness of God's salvation fully offered in Christ. The chaplain stands within and points to this stark contrast, ensuring that both aspects must be acknowledged, accepted and ultimately integrated.

Reference

Shanks, A. (2008), *Against Innocence: Gillian Rose's Reception and Gift of Faith*. London: SCM Press.

Part 5

CHAPLAINS' STORIES – OTHER SECTORS

20

London Luton Airport

MICHAEL BANFIELD

Becoming an airport chaplain was difficult. It required a great deal of thought and prayer because it was something I really wanted to do! Was this the call of God or just a dear wish that linked with one of my greatest interests and life passions? With a group of school friends I had been keen on civil aviation since childhood. Several of us went on to work in aviation, two becoming air traffic controllers, one a pilot and one – me – going to work for an airline. At the same time I was growing as a Christian. Gradually the call to full-time ministry became clear in my early twenties, and aviation was somewhat reluctantly shelved. Three church ministries over 20 years followed theological college, until a quiet personal midlife restlessness began to create a double interest in people at work and in the possibilities of airport chaplaincy.

A door appeared to be opening, was pushed, and I found that I could walk in, first to part-time voluntary chaplaincy and then in 1995 to a full-time ecumenical chaplaincy at London Luton Airport. As this is written I am still there, still feeling called and still finding daily opportunities to serve God's Kingdom in an environment I understand and love.

On one level a commercial airport is a transport hub served by the airport operating company, the airlines and their staff, the provider of air traffic services and all the concessionaires and suppliers. Yet at a deeper level it is far more: it is a very close community. A large airport is almost a city in itself, a place of international exchange where cultures, languages and many and various needs meet and coexist. Airports are full of noise, bustle and, for many passengers and sometimes staff, stress. They are anonymous places that can draw their own population of homeless people, stranded people, aviation enthusiasts and passengers who may be travelling amid any number of needs. Some may be responding to bad news, others are travelling for joyful reunions. Some are on business, some flying to see friends and relatives, others going on holiday. An airport can be a soulless place for the passenger, especially late at night or early in the morning. However, at the same time it is a workplace that inspires great loyalty and camaraderie and becomes a community that may attract several generations of one family to work for one or other company. The aviation industry has a continual buzz about it. All these features and more need to be borne in mind by the chaplain.

Founded in 1987, the chaplaincy team at Luton currently consists of nine volunteer chaplains led by myself as the full-time chaplain. Some of its members are ordained but the majority are lay. Through the team, the chaplaincy has grown with the airport over the last 15 years. When I arrived in 1995 there were about 4,000 staff on site and 1.8 million passengers departing from the airport annually. By 2008 those figures had reached about 8,500 staff and 10 million passengers. Although every day is unique in its opportunities, challenges and experiences, what might a theoretical day in the life of an airport chaplain involve?

Obviously there are admin duties such as answering emails and phone messages, alongside the important task of checking log entries from team members. This helps to gauge the total activity of the chaplaincy and learn of any news or issues on the previous day. Then there is workplace visiting to companies on site and to airport company offices and departments. Through these visits the chaplain becomes known and his or her availability is made clear. They also help understanding of the issues and concerns of those working in the aviation industry (it is also important to keep up to date via reading, Internet sites and aviation news magazines). Such visiting can lead to deeper conversations or visits to the chaplain for pastoral care.

Such a proactive ministry is generally not possible with passengers. Here what is required is a readiness to be called out in support of staff when passengers are stranded or in various special needs. Sometimes a call will come to the terminal building: a passenger has been taken ill or collapsed; or perhaps there has been a death late in the flight, and no time to divert – the aircraft arrives with the deceased still strapped in the seat. Alternatively support might be needed for a pilgrimage group departing to Israel on one of our daily flights to Tel Aviv, or for the charity that sends sick children on wishes to Disney near Paris. Establishing links with passenger services staff, floor walkers, information desks and terminal duty officer teams is vital in order for the awareness of the chaplain's availability to be known. This can best be done by terminal-building walkabouts. It helps this task of establishing a faith-based presence if some identifying clothing is worn, such as a clerical collar or yellow high-visibility tabard or jacket with 'Airport Chaplaincy' clearly signified.

Where a chapel or prayer room exists the chaplain will see it as a responsibility to care for it on behalf of the airport, providing faith literature and perhaps short worship or prayer services. At Luton we have a 30-seat chapel that is 'landside' and a small 'airside' multi-faith prayer room. There is a weekly Christian service in the chapel, announced over the PA system, which either I or another team member leads.

By the end of the day around 100 people, or in large airports many more, may have been met, enquired after and listened to for a few minutes. A chaplaincy presence, influence and ministry will have been shown in various forms for different people – staff, passengers, aircrew, visitors. Some will have had opportunity to share news or concerns or discuss a personal or spiritual issue. In one or two cases real spiritually founded conversations may have ensued in which a sharing of the faith has been possible, though always leaving the other to set the discussion agenda.

Alongside day-to-day issues there are other areas worthy of con-sideration, particularly when establishing chaplaincy at a new site. Is the chaplain a guest or staff team-member? How is the chaplain seen by those being served? How does the chaplain see the role? Whose representative is the chaplain and by whose authority is that ministry carried out? There are different models of airport chaplaincy and different means of financial support/sponsorship. It will be important for the chaplain to link with others exercising the same ministry across the world. There are, therefore, benefits from joining the membership of the professional association for airport chaplains, the IACAC. The chaplain may also be able to play a role in assisting the airport and its local community to have an engaged relationship in which the airport is able to be a good neighbour, despite noise and environmental issues and concerns. Ethical issues, such as staff terms and conditions, global warming/climate change and carbon footprints, may need to be con-sidered and addressed.

When the airport company agrees the need, or perhaps has no existing arrangements elsewhere, the chaplain should become involved in providing a larger team of faith representatives and clergy to act as an emergency response team. This is to provide humanitarian assistance and spiritual support to survivors/evacuees and families/friends in the case of a major incident or accident. The potential importance of this side of the chaplain's work should never be underestimated. It is advisable that the chaplain ask for permission to become a member of the airport's emergency planning group (or similar).

Airport chaplaincy will not suit all types. For the chaplain in a single ministry there may be a degree of loneliness or isolation from the faith community. There will, at times, be a wondering whether and to what extent the ministry achieves the aims of the faith the chaplain represents, since results are not easy to assess. For the full-time chaplain there may be a sense of belonging neither to the Church – or other faith body – nor to the airport. This has to be lived with. But for those God calls, for those constitutionally suited to it, for those able to form and build pastoral relationships with people at work on a long-term basis and for those who have or gain an enthusiasm for the aviation world, this ministry is a high privilege and most satisfying.

21

Manchester United FC*

JOHN BOYERS

It was over 30 years ago that I felt the call of God to offer my time as a chaplain to the local football club in Watford. That came about, and I served the club as a pastoral and spiritual support for about 15 years. This involved giving a day and a half to the staff at the club as part of the commitment of my local church to our community. This service was not with a Baptist tag. I felt I represented 'the Church' as a whole and on their behalf tried to be pastor to a 'football club congregation'. I sought to help people of all faith backgrounds and none. Over many years the club appreciated the involvement. They knew that some people found my presence very helpful, and Watford FC were keen to endorse it in various ways.

Manchester United FC invited me to do a similar job for them full-time in 1987. However, the growth in the Watford church and the impending loss of my assistant minister to another church made such a move impossible at that time. Besides, I did wonder if a full-time chaplain was the best model for Manchester United to establish. They are an influential and bigger club, and I felt the 'Watford model' of chaplaincy – a part-time chaplain giving his time for free – would be more likely to be taken up successfully by other clubs. By 1991 I was working to create an interdenominational body to develop sports chaplaincy provision – Sports Chaplains Offering Resources and Encouragement, or SCORE. Baptist leaders had asked me if I'd be willing to leave local church work to pioneer chaplaincy development in sport ecumenically. The following year Manchester United again asked me to become involved with them, this time on a part-time basis. After much prayer, we moved the family to Manchester and in September 1992 I took on the chaplaincy role at Old Trafford, where I now give two full days per week to providing spiritual and pastoral support.

The work I do with MUFC is very similar to the work done by other sports chaplains throughout the UK. I give an agreed amount

---

* This chapter is a shortened version of an article originally published by *Thinking Faith*, the online journal of the British Jesuits at <www.thinkingfaith.org>.

of time to the club, and my role is very varied. Part of it is building relationships with staff and players across the club so that if they need my help in any way I am not just a name on a piece of paper but someone they know. I get called on to do 'religious' work (perhaps a funeral service, a wedding, a special thanksgiving or a remembrance service), particularly by people who do not have any local church link. I am often contacted informally when someone wants confidential comment or a neutral perspective on a troubling personal issue. SCORE has some 'life-skills' teaching material that looks at issues such as friend-ships, bereavement, bullying, sexual ethics, decision-making, prejudice, privilege and responsibility and so on, and I do some educational work with younger academy players. These lessons help to build positive relationships between players and chaplains. I also share my time with under-16, under-18 and reserve teams – chaplains need to be interested in all teams, not just first teams! Similarly chaplains do not just work with players, so I ensure I am known to staff at the stadium and the offices. I am available to all, 24/7. In the event of an emergency and on match days I have a role as part of the emergency support structures. Finally, I pray for people, for their needs or challenges, for the respon-sibilities they carry – but not for results!

Paul writes in Philippians 2.5–11 about Christ's servanthood. There is great relevance to sports chaplaincy here. It is not about mixing with the famous, getting tickets for games or access to special lounges on match day but about serving. It is about serving all people – the part-time cleaner as much as the international superstar. Chaplains are there not for what they get out of their involvement but for what they contribute to the life of a club or games event. The clergyman who says he wants to be chaplain at Chelsea FC but not chaplain at Brentford FC has an attitude that fails to correspond with the attitude of Christ commended by St Paul. Chaplains are present to serve – with confidentiality, integrity, sensitivity and consistency.

Relationship is at the heart of Christian faith and of sports chaplaincy. His or her contributions can only be optimized if the chaplain is known and trusted and what is on offer understood. Chaplains need to be sensi-tive people. Listening skills are very valuable, as is spiritual discernment. Likewise chaplains need to be what they say they are and do what they say they will do. Sports people are often surrounded by those who want simply to use them or to use a link with them – to promote business, gain tickets or kudos, have photographs or autographs and so on. They see through such people. Chaplains always need to be acting in ways that are congruent with what they say they offer the club and its staff.

Many of the challenges that face a sports chaplain resemble those that anyone who undertakes pastoral work will encounter at some point. How does a Christian work in chaplaincy in a multi-faith world? What problems might face a person working as the sole chaplain in any setting where they are tasked with representing the wider Church rather than just their denomination? But there are also questions that present themselves quite uniquely to those who undertake this particular kind of ministry. Priests/pastors/ministers/vicars have defined roles in their parishes but how does this extend to a wider community role? How can a case for involvement in a sports club be made to congregation or to denomination? From the other direction, what are the characteristics of the sports person or the sports world that the potential chaplain needs to understand? To what extent do we need to understand the environment we seek to serve? How do we come to understand the environment of sports clubs or sports events?

It may also be difficult to find the right person to engage in this particular work. To many the role of chaplain to a sports club might sound like a dream job but does that mean they are right for it? How does the sports-interested person who really does not have the ministry gifting or personality traits to fit easily into sports chaplaincy balance interest with suitability? How does the suitably gifted, trained, understanding individual whom the local club finds very acceptable, who might have major local church responsibilities too, consistently find the time to be chaplain to the staff of the local sports club? SCORE seeks to help those we work with answer questions like these, so that those who find themselves called to this unique ministry are able to be witnesses to the love of Christ for all those they encounter.

22

Community arts in Bensham
and Gateshead

JIM CRAIG

I took up my post as community arts chaplain in the spring of 2005. In 1998 Anthony Gormley's *Angel of the North* had been officially unveiled, and it seemed that the attention of the whole country was focused on Gateshead. Not wanting to rest on their laurels, Gateshead Council went on to trump this success in 2002 with the opening of the Baltic Centre for Contemporary Art, a conversion of a disused flour mill on the Gateshead Quayside. This cultural prowess was fortified in 2004 when the Sage Gateshead opened. The town's renown as the arts capital of the north was complete. It was a great time to be working in Gateshead. However, the response to these initiatives from local people was not universally positive. When regional broadcasters turned out to gauge the public response the results were mixed. They appreciated the fact that the dilapidated Quayside was finally being regenerated but they failed to see how it was anything to do with them.

This started the ball rolling with the arts chaplaincy post. The parishes of Gateshead and Bensham decided to collaborate on a joint bid to secure a stipendiary post for an arts mediator, someone who could bridge the culture gap between those who did and did not take part in the arts. The story of how my job was created is important as it determined the arc that the project was destined to take. I was asked to help make participation in the arts more accessible and that is what I have endeavoured to achieve.

As the post was a completely new one I was allowed to write my own job description. For the first 18 months I charged myself with two duties: to get myself firmly on the radar of the local arts community and to offer creative opportunities to the parishes. Five and a half years on, these duties have remained virtually the same except that I now engage mostly with the wider Gateshead community rather than members of the congregations I cover. This move has happened rather organically. In 2008 I received funding from Awards for All for a project called 'Clarts' (Communities Learning through the Arts). This allowed me to accelerate the development of the arts workshops I was running with community groups. Clarts was specifically chosen as a title for the project because of its colloquial connotations: in the north, to 'get clarty' means to get dirty, and my project was all about persuading people to try their hand at various arts activities without worrying too much about the results. This is the ethos of the arts chaplaincy – as long as you try your best there is no such thing as getting it wrong. My aim was to work with people who would usually run a mile when given the chance to try their hand at painting, dancing, music-making or any arts activity.

I quickly discovered that given the right encouragement people can be incredibly creative. Some are reticent to take part in creative activity because they are afraid of discovering more reasons to consider themselves failures. Sometimes I find myself stepping into the role of counsellor and am amazed at the resolute determination of some people not to risk discovering a hidden talent. Discovering a well of creative talent can be almost a traumatic event if you are convinced you do not have the capacity to produce something beautiful. People who have had their self-confidence battered by years of emotional abuse tend to pride themselves on the useful and practical skills that help them justify their place in the world. Given an opportunity to produce something that is relatively 'useless', they enter a different relationship with themselves. It kickstarts a dialogue with their inner selves that questions their need to define themselves solely by what they achieve. I believe it opens up the possibility of grace. This surely is a way the Church can become good news to communities who have no knowledge of the love of God. We need to remind people that they are worthy enough to be entrusted with creative activities, while providing them with a supportive environment in which they can explore the creativity they have often denied themselves.

From the beginning the Clarts workshops were received well by the groups I worked with. Although I am willing to work with schools and youth groups, I have always tried to prioritize working with local people who do not particularly show up on the council's radar. People responded well to the invitation to take part in professional arts activities in the safe surroundings of their own community spaces. As the project was founded on an ethos of accessibility, I thought it imperative that the workshops be delivered on home soil rather than in churches. If it was good enough for Jesus to seek the lost sheep of Israel proactively, what right had I to erect further barriers and expect people to turn up at a venue that was unfamiliar to them?

There is nothing orthodox about being an arts chaplain. I have not made a supreme effort to use Clarts as a means of inviting people to church services – a difficult task even if I thought it valid. I cover three churches in two parishes, both of which have their own clergy, and while

I have invited members of the congregations to take part in workshops, I have never received the same response that the projects garner in the wider community. This perceived lack of interest may be partly down to the infrequency with which I visit the different congregations: on the Sunday rota for both parishes I only visit each congregation once a month. However, I will always be slightly disappointed that it has been harder to get the churches to take up an invitation to take part in my workshops. I have come to realize that the church leaders of the past spent too much time cultivating a spirit of resigned commitment to the business of running a church. In an age when the same small number of volunteers is being leant on to undertake an ever increasing list of tasks, there is something radical about inviting Christians to take part in activities that are thoroughly unproductive.

I see my ministry as one that sits parallel with the itinerant story-telling of Jesus. When he was faced with a crowd he always had a story to tell. Sometimes he became the story through the enactment of signs and wonders. Either way the effect was that these creative events enabled listeners to step momentarily outside the protocol-driven world they inhabited into a world of imaginative grace. These story-events provided people with a small distraction, which lowered their intellectual guard. Few of us are prepared to give up the limited world-views that drive our inner lives. Jesus possessed a masterful integrity and demanded no conventional response to the parables he told. People were entrusted to return to him, to ask further questions about the Kingdom in their own time. This is what the arts chaplaincy should be all about – entrusting people with a creativity that has the power to remind them that we are made in the image of God.

Stipendiary arts chaplains in the Church of England will always remain controversial. Every now and again I realize that I am looked down upon by certain members of the diocese who feel that the funding for my post would be better spent on a more traditional parish appointment. However, I feel that the Church is playing a dangerous game if it dares to forget the Sabbath principle. As Jesus says in Mark 2.27, 'The sabbath was made for humankind, and not humankind for the sabbath.' We run the risk of short-changing the people of God if we are always prioritizing work over play. I am convinced that as a member of the clergy I can only demand one thing from my congregations, and that is that they give their whole selves to God. God does not just want us for our financial skills, nor just to be good wardens or sides-people or Readers; he wants us to offer 'our souls and bodies, to be a living sacrifice'. If my tenure as arts chaplain comes to an end tomorrow, this will be the lesson that will inspire and enrich any future parish ministry for the rest of my life.

Part 6

THEOLOGICAL REFLECTIONS

23

Responding to diversity: chaplaincy in a multi-faith context

ANDREW TODD

Chaplaincy in a multi-faith context

Until comparatively recently chaplaincy has been an almost exclusively Christian activity, dominated in England and Wales by the Anglican churches. The role of Anglican chaplains has often been seen as an aspect of the role of the established Church, extending the ministry of the parish church into hospitals, workplaces, industry and so on. The clearest example of this is the 1952 Prison Act, which still requires that each prison in England and Wales have an Anglican chaplain. A further example of the way in which chaplaincy has represented an aspect of establishment is provided by documents accompanying the foundation of the NHS, which both draw specific attention to the 'spiritual needs' of patients and staff and speak of the need to appoint chaplains (Orchard, 2000). However, in this case chaplains were to be of different denominations. This signals one of the ways in which chaplaincy has developed in the second half of the twentieth century and first decade of the twenty-first. Christian chaplaincy has become increasingly ecumenical, marked by greater numbers of ministers from denominations and churches other than Anglicanism working as chaplains and taking responsibility as lead or coordinating chaplains.

This development has been but a precursor to, and an element of, the wider development considered here, which includes two interrelated strands. One is the development of multi-faith chaplaincy, understood as an increase in the number and roles of chaplains from faiths other than Christianity. The second is the development of chaplaincy that reaches beyond traditional religious roles and boundaries to those of other belief positions (such as humanism) and those whose philosophy or beliefs are derived or developed in more individual ways. Sometimes known as 'generic' chaplaincy, this approach is a response not only to religious diversity but also to a wider diversity of ways in which humans find meaning in and for their lives. Such an approach is designated in healthcare as 'spiritual' rather than 'religious' care. It is typically defined

in terms such as those provided by the National Institute for Clinical
Excellence (NICE) guidelines on palliative care for adults with cancer:

> Listening to the patient's experience and the questions that may arise;
> affirming the patient's humanity; protecting the patient's dignity, self worth
> and identity; ensuring that spiritual care is offered as an integral part of
> an holistic approach to health, encompassing psychological, spiritual, social
> and emotional care, and within the framework of the patient's beliefs or
> philosophy of life.   (NICE, 2004)

If such developments in chaplaincy might be described as 'interfaith',
then that might almost be taken to have two meanings: the usual
meaning of interaction between those of different faiths; and a less
usual meaning of working with those philosophies that develop in
the interstices of the patchwork of faiths and beliefs to be found in
contemporary society.

An area of chaplaincy provision that illustrates the development in
both faith-specific and 'generic' directions is that of chaplaincy spaces
for reflection, meditation, prayer and worship, now to be found in
such settings as hospitals, universities and airports. There are a number
of conundrums faced by those responsible for the provision of multi-
faith spaces as replacements or additional resources for the historic
provision of Christian chapels. These cluster in two areas: that of how
the particular practices of different faith groups can be provided for;
and that of how spaces can be open to a wide range of users in such a
way that they feel comfortable in the space.

Under the first heading are questions about provision of a single space
in which different traditions are accommodated or multiple spaces set
aside for different traditions. In the more usual scenario (often because
of budget constraints) of the shared single space, questions follow about
the accommodation of different traditions' artefacts and sacred texts and
allocation of use for shared worship, prayer or meditation. This is made
more of a challenge because the need for space set aside for religious
practice is not evenly distributed across traditions. Some faiths (such as
Islam) generate a sense of the importance of regular corporate use of
such space. Followers of other traditions, which emphasize individual
practice, will be more occasional users.

Under the second heading, questions arise about whether particular
artefacts will offend those of other traditions and positions, with con-
sequent questions about whether permanent artefacts should be kept
to a minimum; or of screening or storage to hide them when not in use.
Further issues arise when seeking to offer an inclusive space because of
the different ways of approaching prayer spaces that belong to different
traditions: with shoes on or off; with the hope of areas segregated by

gender or not; with the expectation of particular items of furniture or of a space empty of furniture.

Social, cultural and political contexts

In order to locate the developments in chaplaincy outlined above and to offer some explanation of what has driven them, we now turn to some key social, cultural and political developments that provide a backdrop and wider framework. Whereas ecumenical chaplaincy may be located to some extent in relation to earlier British debates about religious toleration and freedom for different Christian denominations, multi-faith and generic chaplaincy require a larger, more contemporary context. Among other possibilities, three interlinked and complex aspects of contemporary society are of particular significance.

The first of these is pluralism. In keeping with Beckford's (2003) clarification of this concept, this is taken to refer first to the fact of pluralism, or more particularly that British culture now includes a diversity of religious and philosophical positions. Clearly chaplaincy is responding to this situation of increased diversity. Second, pluralism is understood as signifying the increasing public acceptance or recognition of religious diversity. Prima facie, multi-faith chaplaincy appears to be in keeping with such an acceptance. However, specific examples, considered below, suggest that this might not be such a coherent picture as first presumed. Given the power differentials between chaplains of different faiths, writing in 2003 Beckford was cautious about whether prison chaplaincy demonstrated pluralism. More recently, Gilliat-Ray (2008) gives grounds for a greater optimism as she discusses the growing role of Muslim chaplains in prisons. The third sense that pluralism can have, and that Beckford identified as the only sense in which he would use the term, is that of 'normative commitment'. Beckford describes this as 'support for the moral or political value of widening the public acceptance of religions'. Whether such a public commitment is represented in the changing policy relating to chaplaincy is at this stage an entirely open question.

The second area relates to ways in which pluralism has been recognized, safeguarded and – at least to some extent – promoted through equality-and-diversity policy and legislation. Of key importance to chaplaincy are:

- the 1998 Human Rights Act, which provides a key link with the European Convention on Human Rights;
- race relations legislation up to and including the 2000 Race Relations (Amendment) Act, which has provided for religious discrimination to be addressed in relation to ethnicity;

- the more recent 2003 Employment Equality (Religion or Belief) Regulations, which addressed questions of religious discrimination in a way that was independent of ethnicity;
- the Equality Act 2010, which drew together the different areas of anti-discrimination law, including that relating to religion and belief.

Thus, for example, the establishment of the category of spiritual care in the context of the NHS may clearly be located, in relation to equality-and-diversity policy, as part of a drive to ensure that all patients (and indeed staff) may be provided for equally.

It would be strange to mention equality and diversity without at least touching on policy that deals with some of the limits of tolerance and freedom of expression. Government's search for 'community cohesion' and for 'shared values' is one such area. The other key area is government response to violent extremism, especially the Prevent Agenda. This is discussed below in relation to specific provision designed to realize this policy through the work of prison chaplaincy. The search for social integration, not least in the face of cultural conflict, can certainly touch chaplains. For example, the report from the Department for Innovation, Universities and Skills on promoting good relations on campus (2005) envisaged university chaplains as a resource for the promotion of cohesion on higher education campuses. As a further example, the development of chaplaincy in further education sits squarely within the above policy areas. As is made clear by a report produced by the Learning and Skills Improvement Service (2010), chaplaincy is integral to the provision to learners of spiritual, moral, social and cultural support. Noticeably the document locates the recent development of multi-faith chaplaincy in this sector of education within the frames of both equality and diversity and social cohesion.

The third aspect of the relationship between religion, spirituality and society is the dynamic involving society, individuals and institutional religion. There is considerable interest in whether institutional religion is giving way to rather more individualized, eclectic expressions of spirituality. In the UK this has been explored through the Kendal Project, which identified a growth in holistic forms of spiritual expression over against a decline in institutional religion in the Cumbrian town of Kendal. One thesis presented by Heelas and Woodhead (2005) is that this represents a 'subjective turn' within contemporary culture. Working at the same questions, Davie (2007) points to both the 'consumerist' choice to embrace aspects of religion and spirituality that offer something experiential, or 'feel-good' (including within fundamentalist religious contexts), and also to continued attachment to religious institutions based on latent belief and nominal membership. She further suggests that the boundaries between these two phenomena are far from absolute.

Clearly, such issues are of considerable significance for the study of chaplaincy. As will already be apparent, chaplains work increasingly with individual 'spiritual' or indeed 'religious' questions. At the same time they exist within complex institutional relationships both with their faith communities and with their host or employing organization. The above issues are now explored within three case studies taken from areas of public sector chaplaincy: the military, prisons and healthcare. A key reason for choosing these particular aspects of chaplaincy is that because they operate within the sphere of public life, they are directly driven by the public policy referred to above, and to some extent their future depends on their compliance with such policy.

Case study 1 – Army chaplaincy: between ecumenical and multi-faith chaplaincy

Army chaplains are the subject of dual command in the British Army. They are commanded primarily by the Royal Army Chaplains' Department (RAChD) and secondarily by the commanding officer of the unit with which they serve. Commissioned, they hold equivalent rank to other commissioned officers but are non-combatants and do not carry arms. Currently all commissioned chaplains are Christian, belonging to a wide variety of Christian churches and denominations. Their role is defined in terms of providing spiritual leadership, moral guidance and pastoral care.

Chaplains come from a number of Christian 'sending churches'. Two terms in common usage among Army chaplains illustrate the way in which chaplains from different Christian traditions work together. One is their commitment to an 'all-souls ministry', so that each chaplain has a commitment to minister to any soldier, irrespective of that soldier's beliefs, albeit from within a Christian model of pastoral care. Thus they offer 'pastoral support for all who seek it, whatever their religion, beliefs or background might be' (RAChD, 2010a). To a degree, this acknowledges and respects that soldiers hold a diversity of beliefs. The second term is 'convergence', which refers to the process by which all commissioned chaplains have been brought under a single command structure within the RAChD. This now includes Roman Catholic chaplains, who previously had a parallel structure. Evidence of the success of 'convergence' is provided by senior chaplains who are not Anglican. In 2010, although the serving Chaplain General was an Anglican, his predecessor was a Methodist minister and the Deputy Chaplain General was a Baptist minister. This is, however, still very much a Christian model of chaplaincy, illustrated by the current Chaplain General's 'Plan for Mission', which articulates the work of the RAChD in terms of a Christian theology of mission.

This approach to chaplaincy is held in tension with a more pro-actively multi-faith one expressed on the RAChD official website (2010b): 'The wealth and diversity of experience that each chaplain brings helps create a department that is continually evolving at the cutting edge of multi-denominational and multi-faith ministry.' In practice this is realized largely in the work of 'world faith' chaplains, which the Army shares with the Navy and the RAF. The tri-service policy on their role is presented as follows on the RAF chaplaincy site:

> According to statistics published in July 2005 most service men and women share a Christian faith (183,000). In addition 220 are Buddhists, 56 Jewish, 230 Hindus, 305 Muslims and 90 Sikhs. In 2005 the MOD recruited four chaplains from these major world religions to help enhance our spiritual care to all personnel. These new chaplains work alongside the existing Commissioned Chaplains and our honorary Jewish Chaplain, Rabbi Malcolm Weisman.   (RAF Chaplains' Branch, 2010)

In part this multi-faith model is justified in terms of providing equal opportunity, on a proportional basis, for all soldiers; there being only small numbers of faiths other than Christianity. However, the fact that the 'world faith' chaplains are civilians recruited by the Ministry of Defence excludes them from full participation in forces chaplaincy. Further, their working model is different from that of commissioned Army chaplains. Rather than being attached to a particular unit and serving all soldiers in that unit, world faith chaplains serve those of their own faith and work across the three armed services. There is speculation among Army chaplains that there will be commissioned world faith chaplains in the future, but there appears to be no concrete proposal at present to implement such a change.

While numbers make it difficult (in the figures given above fewer than 0.5 per cent belong to other faiths), this might be described as a limited accommodation of other faiths with limited signs of a 'normative commitment' to the value of religious diversity. One of the things that may constrain the military approach to religious diversity is the par-ticular moral role of the Army (and indeed Navy and RAF) chaplain. In each service there is an expectation that chaplains will contribute to moral training, to the formation of personnel in the core values of their service. This represents an aspect of a deliberate policy of maintaining a distinct, cohesive military identity, with a perceived stronger commitment to 'traditional' values than is to be found in contemporary society and an attachment to a Christian heritage (Deakin, 2008).

Case study 2 – Prison chaplaincy: a multi-faith model serving cohesion

Reflecting the different demographics involved, prison chaplaincy in England and Wales provides a much more thoroughgoing example of multi-faith chaplaincy. This is currently directed by the Prison Standing Order (PSO) 4550 (HM Prison Service, 2000), underpinned by the prison Performance Standard 51. PSO 4550 makes clear that the Prison Service recognizes the rights of prisoners to practise their religion; to participate in worship and other religious activities; and to receive pastoral care. Primary responsibility for making provision for these rights to be met lies with prison chaplains working in multi-faith teams. PSO 4550 makes provision for: appointment of chaplains/ministers; religious registration; places of worship; corporate worship; pastoral care; religious education classes; religious observance (such as festivals); diet, dress and religious artefacts. It further contains some detail about how these might apply in the case of different religions. It ought to be said that this does not ignore the needs of those who do not espouse a particular faith – even if they are still described by the category 'nil religion'. Chaplains' 'statutory duties', shared today by chaplains of different faiths, include the care of all prisoners irrespective of belief, for example, involving meeting all prisoners new to the chaplain's prison. Governance of prison chaplaincy includes the Prison Service Chaplaincy Council, which replaced an earlier body in 2003 and which includes faith advisers representing major world faiths (Buddhism, Hinduism, Islam, Judaism, Church of Jesus Christ of Latter-Day Saints (Mormon), Sikhism, Paganism). It further includes a Chaplain General and other senior chaplains, including one Muslim, employed as civil servants to direct prison chaplaincy within the National Offender Management Service.

In one sense the development of Muslim prison chaplaincy illustrates the trend from the norm of an Anglican prison chaplain, envisaged by the 1952 Prison Act, to multi-faith teams. Against the background of an increase in the Muslim prison population to 9,930, some 12 per cent of the total prisoner population in England and Wales, numbers of Muslim chaplains have also grown (Hansard, 2009). The first full-time Muslim chaplain was appointed in 2003. In 2009 there were nearly 200 Muslim chaplains (approximately 20 per cent of the total number of chaplains), 38 working full-time (theyworkforyou.com, 2009). However, interpretation of these figures is not straightforward. In one sense this is a positive equal-opportunity response to a change in the religious diversity among prisoners, although the questions raised by Beckford and Gilliat-Ray, discussed above, need to be taken into account. At another level, however, the increase in the number of Muslim chaplains is also a response to concerns about extremism. The parliamentary answer of September 2009, referred to above in relation to the number of Muslim prisoners, specifically connected addressing violent extremism and radicalization with Muslim chaplaincy:

> As part of the National Offender Management Service's programme of work to address the risks associated with violent extremism and radicalisation, a series of briefings, written material, and training events have been delivered at both national and local level to a range of operational and non-operational staff working across prisons and probation, including Muslim chaplains. (Hansard, 2009)

Further, one of the specific briefs of the Prison Service Extremism Unit, established in 2007, is to provide support for Muslim chaplains. There is some suggestion that the Prevent Agenda has shaped the 'normative commitment' to pluralism, undue attention being given to Muslim chaplaincy in comparison with other world faiths. Further research (such as that being carried out at Cardiff University by the Centre for Chaplaincy Studies and the Centre for the Study of Islam in the UK) is necessary to confirm this.

Case study 3 – Healthcare chaplaincy: multi-faith and generic models in dialogue with the question of professionalization

In healthcare chaplaincy there appear to be two strands to the response to working in a multi-faith context. Like prison chaplaincy, healthcare chaplains have broadened their response to diverse religious affiliation among patients and staff through the inclusion within teams of chaplains of world faiths other than Christianity, including as lead chaplains. The extent of this development is difficult to judge. A recent report suggested that of 425 full-time healthcare chaplains in the NHS only 8 were from a faith other than Christianity – in all cases Muslim – and that of some 3,000 part-time chaplains only 200 were from faiths other than Christianity (Church of England, 2010).

The second strand of healthcare responses to a multi-faith context relates to the development of 'spiritual' care as something distinct from 'religious' care. As articulated within the NHS, spiritual care is offered both by chaplains and other healthcare professionals (notably nurses). It is specifically designed to include those who do not espouse a particular faith. Spiritual care is directed towards the spiritual needs of all. As suggested by the NICE guidelines quoted earlier, spirituality is understood to be an aspect of humanity relating to beliefs and philosophy, which is independent of religion (although some people will express their spirituality in a religious way).

Some caution needs to be exercised in evaluating spiritual care. Swift (2009) offers a picture, rooted in ethnographic as well as documentary research, of the use of the phrase as an accommodation to the changing context of healthcare that does not necessarily change the actual practice of engaging with patients and staff. He points both to ill-defined and contested understandings of spiritual care to be found in healthcare literature – especially relating to nursing practice – and to the lack of a distinctive practice of such care in chaplaincy. In relation to the latter, his 'autoethnography' – ethnographic study of his own chaplaincy work – reveals his own practice of spiritual care to be resourced from and shaped by his own Christian tradition and training. Further, he sets the particular situation in healthcare within a wider understanding that the distinction between religion and spirituality is overplayed; that spirituality may be less a shift away from religion, more a reaction against religious authority.

Swift is right in thus identifying a gap between the rhetoric of spiritual care and the practice. Nonetheless the phrase has become firmly embedded in the discourse of healthcare chaplaincy. It thus acts as a political driver that is beginning to move chaplaincy in the direction of a more wholehearted response to diversity. Such moves are seen in current debates and research about how 'spiritual' need may be assessed, and in the way in which the capabilities and competencies of healthcare chaplaincy are defined (NHS Education Scotland, 2008). It would appear that chaplains – and other healthcare professionals – are in the process of talking a new area of practice into existence.

This is further illustrated by a phrase in common usage among health-care chaplains to describe work in relation to spiritual rather than specific religious need – 'generic chaplaincy'. While the meaning of the phrase is unclear and contested, it acts as a useful shorthand term for the purposes of this chapter, standing here for chaplains' aspirations to respond to diversity of belief, and for their emerging practice of spiritual care. This approach is expressed in terms of a flexible approach, which involves listening to, discerning and responding to the needs expressed by patients, relatives and staff. This requires, both in theory and practice, consider-able openness on the part of the chaplain as well as the wisdom to know when a particular spiritual need requires referral to another practitioner with expertise in a particular area of belief or religious practice.

The development of a generic approach to chaplaincy and of the concept of spiritual care has an impact on the understanding of religious care, which is not only distinguished from but also located within the broader category of spiritual care. The notion of spiritual need, independent from religious need, creates a universal aim for healthcare chaplaincy. Further, the rhetoric of spiritual care as the umbrella for religious care (where religions are seen as ways of expressing spirituality) also relativizes religion, reducing the privilege given to any one religion or to those who identify as religious over those who do not. This is not only about responding to spiritual and religious needs in their own right. Chaplains' own work, and their education and leadership of other healthcare practitioners in the practice of spiritual care, offer evidence of a commitment to spirituality and religion as a valued contribution to holistic care and the well-being of staff, patients, families and carers.

Questions arising for the future of chaplaincy

On the above analysis, healthcare chaplaincy appears to have embraced pluralism as 'normative commitment' to a greater extent than military or prison chaplaincy. This is perhaps significant. One might suggest that for both military and prison chaplaincy there is a greater institutional drive towards a coherent model of chaplaincy. In the armed services this has to do with the chaplain's role in maintaining the moral identity of military personnel – promoting core values that are perceived by the military as distancing the organization from wider society. In prisons it appears that the security agenda, and concern to address violent extremism, have a part to play in shaping prison chaplaincy. Healthcare provision is perhaps driven more straightforwardly by the need to respond to patient need and choice, as expressed in the 2010 NHS Constitution: 'You have the right to make choices about your NHS care and to information to support these choices. The options available to you will develop over time and depend on your individual needs' (Department of Health, 2010).

So far I have largely focused on the practice of chaplaincy; on what chaplains are doing to respond to diversity, on changing structures, for example, or the use of sacred space. This is in keeping with a fitting pragmatism, characteristic of much chaplaincy, that is driven by a concern to respond pastorally to human need, hope, aspiration and perplexity. However, this particular focus can hide some of the more theoretical questions raised by and often addressed within chaplaincy in transition. A number of these questions are rooted in the fact that chaplaincy's heritage is a Christian one. The inherited language is Christian, including the term 'chaplain' itself and key concepts such as 'pastoral care'. Further, the knowledge base for chaplaincy developed during much of the twentieth century is shaped by Christian theology, specifically by pastoral and/or practical theology and the particular practice of theological reflection. This has given rise to models of chaplaincy that fit within those traditions, such as the chaplain as 'pastor', 'priest', or 'prophet'. This heritage has been adopted and adapted by chaplains of faiths other than Christianity and also modified in the light of secular viewpoints. But there remains some work to be done in developing a knowledge base that fully supports chaplaincy, as it responds to diverse spiritual and religious needs.

The directions that such developments might take are dependent to a large extent on key questions implicit in the analysis of responses to diversity offered earlier in the chapter. First, how far chaplaincy in all its variety will continue to expand in a multi-faith direction, responding to the particularity of religious and other beliefs and increasing the range of its belief-specific provision, including the range of beliefs represented by chaplains. Second, how far it will develop in ways that seek to offer a greater flexibility of response to diversity, involving each chaplain being prepared to work with an increasing spectrum of belief and practice. Almost certainly both directions will be a necessary aspect of the evolution of chaplaincy. However, the balance between them is likely to play a key part in the extent and characteristics of chaplaincy's sense of shared identity within a multi-faith context.

Thus in relation to chaplaincy's knowledge-base – the development of more theoretical understandings of chaplaincy rooted in its practice – there already exists a tension between the two directions. On the one hand, there is some debate currently about the theology of chaplaincy in a multi-faith context. While acknowledging that the word 'theology' is itself Christian, chaplains of faiths other than Christianity are engaging in reflection that links chaplaincy with their faith texts, traditions and practices. For example, Muslim chaplains are asking what a Muslim theology of chaplaincy might look like. Chaplains from different traditions, working within the wider field of interfaith dialogue, are exploring (at least at local level) whether and how different faith-based understandings of chaplaincy can be brought into conversation with each other. The range of issues therefore includes theologies of chaplaincy appropriate to different faiths and theologies that support dialogue between faith-specific approaches.

On the other hand, more generic approaches to the practice-generated theory of chaplaincy are being developed. These might be rooted in an understanding of 'reflective practice' shared with other fields of professional practice. As an example of how this gives rise to knowledge supportive of chaplaincy, healthcare chaplains and others are grappling with spiritual need. As indicated above, a particular question of the moment is how such need may be assessed and measured. This fits within a wider model of healthcare reflective practice, which considers how practitioners, including chaplains, shape their therapeutic intervention around such assessment – as well as around subsequent evaluation – as part of the culture of 'evidence-based practice'. Both the specific concept of chaplaincy assessment and intervention, and the wider frame of reflective practice, are key components of recent approaches to the competencies and capabilities necessary for healthcare chaplaincy, such as those previously referred to developed by NHS Education Scotland.

The balance and interconnection between the two directions taken already by chaplaincy reflection on practice will affect other areas. Notable among these is education for chaplains, both in preparation for the role and as part of continuing professional development. Thus a shift in the balance towards a generic educational approach, grounded in professional reflective practice, might well offer a coherent package of education. But a reduction in the component of chaplaincy education that has to do with theology or faith traditions would significantly constrain the faith-based resources on which chaplaincy has hitherto drawn to a considerable extent. The risk here is that this might reduce or even remove a key component of the knowledge that distinguishes chaplaincy as a specialism with a distinctive contribution to make to the chaplain's host organization.

The imaginative way forward is to seek further integration and mutual critique between the approaches chaplains share with other professionals and insights they draw from different faiths. However, this can be something of a challenge to a contemporary secular view that faith-based reflection can only properly support 'religious' practice rather than the wider 'spiritual' quest. This view seems to be grounded in a concern that religions will seek to impose their particular approach to questions of faith and belief on others.

Particular insights from interfaith dialogue suggest that, in practice, religious traditions may sometimes, at least, have a rather more open approach to offering their insights into the human condition and human flourishing, and to learning from the insights of others. Such openness might be seen in the practice of 'scriptural reasoning' shared by groups of Muslims, Christians and Jews who seek to work together at the interpretation of their sacred texts. It might also be seen in the dialogue about meditative and contemplative practice shared by Buddhists, Christians and others. Further, it may be that chaplains are good at understanding a broad diversity of spiritualities precisely because they have explored the spirituality of their own faith tradition; and that it is this that provides the resources for broad, open conversation about human, spiritual questions of hope, reconciliation or well-being in which generations of chaplains have engaged, while respecting the autonomy of their 'clients'.

As indicated above, at issue is the shared identity of chaplaincy within a multi-faith, multicultural setting. Too great an emphasis on faith-specific provision not only risks competition for scarce resources but also a lack of professional coherence; too great a weight placed on that coherence risks a loss of distinctiveness, rooted in the riches of multiple faith traditions. A balance is necessary, rooted in interfaith dialogue between traditions but offering an interfaith chaplaincy that is able to support those whose spiritual questions are not located within the boundaries of those traditions. Addressing this challenge is vital not only to the identity but also to the legitimacy of chaplaincy. In prison chaplaincy, for example, the established pattern of Anglican chaplaincy has been a vehicle for the development of a multi-faith approach. But that can only be a transitional arrangement. In the end chaplaincy – not only in prisons but in every domain – needs a public legitimacy firmly grounded in its response to diversity and in the ability to respond both with a professional openness to human questions of meaning and identity, however they are expressed, and to the particular needs presented by the practices of identified faith and belief traditions.

References

Beckford, J. A. (2003), *Social Theory and Religion*. Cambridge: Cambridge University Press.

Church of England (2010), *Healthcare Chaplaincy and the Church of England: A Review of the Work of the Hospital Chaplaincies Council*, available at <nhs-chaplaincy-spiritualcare.org.uk/HCC%20Review%20-%20Final%2031.3.10.pdf> [accessed February 2011].

Davie, G. (2007), *The Sociology of Religion*. London: Sage.

Deakin, S. (2008), 'Education in an Ethos at the Royal Military Academy Sandhurst', in Robinson, P., De Lee, N. and Carrick, D. (eds), *Ethics Education in the Military*. Aldershot: Ashgate.

Department for Innovation, Universities and Skills (DIUS) (2005), *Promoting Good Campus Relations: Fostering Shared Values and Preventing Violent Extremism in Universities and Higher Education Colleges*, available at <www.bis.gov.uk/assets/biscore/corporate/migratedd/publications/e/extremismhe.pdf> [accessed April 2010].

Department of Health (2010), *The NHS Constitution for England*, available at <www.dh.gov.uk/en/Publicationsandstatistics/Publications/PublicationsPolicy AndGuidance/DH_113613> [accessed April 2010].

Gilliat-Ray, S. (2008), 'From "Visiting Minister" to "Muslim Chaplain": The Growth of Muslim Chaplaincy in Britain, 1970–2007', in Barker, E. (ed.), *The Centrality of Religion in Social Life: Essays in Honour of James A. Beckford*. Aldershot: Ashgate.

Hansard (2009), *House of Commons Hansard Written Answers for 01 Sep 2009 (pt 0002)*, available at <www.parliament.the-stationery-office.co.uk/pa/cm200809/cmhansrd/cm090901/text/90901w0002.htm> [accessed April 2010].

Heelas, P. and Woodhead, L. (2005), *The Spiritual Revolution: Why Religion is Giving Way to Spirituality*. Oxford: Blackwell.

HM Prison Service (2000), *PSO 4550: Religion Manual*, available at <pso.hmprison service.gov.uk/PSO_4550_religion_manual.doc> [accessed April 2010].

Learning and Skills Improvement Service (2010), *Planning and Delivering Spiritual, Moral, Social and Cultural (SMSC) Support in the Learning and Skills Sector: Guidance for Learning and Skills Providers*, available at <www.lsis.org.uk/Documents/Publications/SMSC%20Web.pdf> [accessed October 2010].

NHS Education Scotland (2008), *Spiritual and Religious Care Capabilities and Competences for Healthcare Chaplains*, available at <www.nes.scot.nhs.uk/media/3738/010308capabilities_and_competences_for_healthcare_chaplains.pdf> [accessed February 2011].

NICE (2004), *Improving Supportive and Palliative Care for Adults with Cancer: The Manual*, available at <www.nice.org.uk/guidance/csgsp/guidance/pdf/English> [accessed April 2010].

Orchard, H. (2000), *Hospital Chaplaincy: Modern, Dependable?* Sheffield: Sheffield Academic Press/Lincoln Theological Institute.

RAChD (2010a), *The Role of Army Chaplains*, available at <www.army.mod.uk/chaplains/role/default.aspx> [accessed April 2010].

RAChD (2010b), *Royal Army Chaplains' Department*, available at <www.army.mod.uk/chaplains/chaplains.aspx> [accessed April 2010].

RAF Chaplains' Branch (2010), *World Faiths*, available at <www.raf.mod.uk/chaplains/whoweare/worldfaiths.cfm> [accessed April 2010].

Swift, C. (2009), *Hospital Chaplaincy in the Twenty-first Century: The Crisis of Spiritual Care on the NHS*. Farnham: Ashgate.

theyworkforyou.com (2009), *Prisons: Muslim Chaplains: 3 Mar 2009: Written Answers and Statements*, available at <www.theyworkforyou.com/wrans/?id=2009-03-03a.143.0> [accessed April 2010].

24

The role and skills of a chaplain

MARK NEWITT

Introduction

Given the extraordinary range of contexts in which chaplains work (the stories told in the first part of this book range from academia's ivory towers to Afghan sand; from bedside vigils to community arts projects), it might be thought nearly impossible to describe the role carried out by a chaplain, let alone the skills required. However, if you take a look at the job descriptions for a range of chaplaincy posts you will see similar phrases cropping up. To give a few examples:

- Pastoral and spiritual care
  - 'provide spiritual and pastoral care' (university)
  - 'provide spiritual leadership and pastoral care' (prison)
  - 'provide spiritual, moral and pastoral support' (Army)
- Leading worship
  - 'co-ordinate appropriate in-house religious services' (hospice)
  - 'lead the spiritual, devotional and worship life of the school' (school)
  - 'plan and lead worship and prayer' (prison)
- Education/training
  - 'chaplains also play an ongoing role in the training of serving personnel' (RAF)
  - 'contribute to training programmes and materials for staff and volunteers' (prison)
  - 'contribute to training and development programmes and to research, to increase, particularly among staff, knowledge and understanding of spiritual needs and skill in meeting them' (mental health)

These job descriptions are clearly broad-brush and do not give any indication of how they are enacted in the day-by-day life of different chaplains. Drawing on personal experience and the stories told in the earlier parts of this book, this chapter attempts to paint a more detailed picture. Before doing so there is merit in exploring the definitions of some of the terms mentioned above, in particular spirituality and pastoral care. There are perhaps as many different definitions of spirituality as there are books on the subject – within this book Andrew Todd (Chapter 23) quotes from NICE guidelines and Lance Blake (Chapter 12) provides one from Murray and Zentner. I do not intend to create yet another but it is worth noting their change and development over time. Koenig (2008) traces this in an article that raises concerns over diverse and poorly defined definitions of spirituality within health research. He suggests that, in what he terms the 'traditional-historical' understanding, spirituality was originally used only in relation to a subset of deeply religious people, such as ascetics and monks. In this model, religion and the secular are seen as distinct and different sources of human values, meaning and purpose. Today however, he argues, the meaning of spirituality has expanded not only to subsume religion and include positive indicators of mental health as part of its definition but also to embrace secular sources. In this definition everyone, including atheists and agnostics, is viewed as having a spirituality. To avoid confusion chaplains must be clear about how they define spirituality and also about how the organization they work for understands the term.

With regard to pastoral care it is important to differentiate between pastoral care and pastoral counselling. Although there can be a considerable degree of overlap in the skills used in each domain, there is a key difference in the way that boundaries are structured. In pastoral counselling the relationship is based around an explicitly agreed, firm set of boundaries. However, in pastoral care, as often seen in the stories in Parts 1–5, boundaries are typically left unspoken and are more flexible. This does not mean that pastoral care is inferior to pastoral counselling. Lyall argues that far from being a lightweight version of counselling, pastoral care should be seen as a discipline in its own right. He sets out his definition of it in some detail, and it is worth reproducing the opening paragraph:

> Pastoral care involves the establishment of a relationship or relationships whose purpose may encompass support in a time of trouble and personal and/or spiritual growth through deeper understanding of oneself, others, and/or God. Pastoral care will have at its heart the affirmation of meaning and worth of persons and will endeavour to strengthen their ability to respond creatively to whatever life brings. (Lyall, 2001)

The work of a chaplain

This definition matches well with many of the descriptions of the work done in the chaplains' stories in the earlier parts of this book. Linking the definition with reflections on a case study, elsewhere I have suggested that a key role of a hospital chaplain is the task of accompanying people through times of transition (Newitt, 2010). The evidence of the stories here is that despite the vastly different contexts in which they operate, many chaplains would recognize this description.

Whether it is termed walking alongside, being a companion or in other closely related terms, most of the contributors speak of accompanying others. Similarly the theme of transition recurs frequently, be it offering hope of transformation, facilitating a journey of exploration or helping people find nurturing and rejuvenation. Within healthcare the chaplain's context is that of change – supporting people as they are restored to health, adapt to impaired physical function or come to terms with their own or a loved one's mortality. In the same way, a good argument can be made that processes of transition lie at the heart of prisons (rehabilitation) and education (formation). Beyond this, in all sectors changes caused by entering and leaving, beginnings and endings can create times of difficulty and challenge through which people may want help adjusting. Ruth Hake, on RAF chaplaincy (Chapter 1), graphically describes the complex feelings evoked in attempting to readjust to being back home after a tour of duty. It is noticeable here that as part of their statutory duties, prison chaplains see every new prisoner admitted. Forces chaplains are likewise an integral part of the initial training of recruits. So as they befriend, journeying with people through the challenges and changes life throws at them, what are the tools and skills a chaplain needs?

Attentive listeners

The first set of competencies can be grouped under the term counselling skills. Showing empathy and unconditional positive regard enables the quick development of trust. Similarly skills associated with active listening enable people to tell their stories and engage in conversation. In relation to supporting through transitions it is interesting to note, as Hugh Shilson-Thomas does (Chapter 9), that the word conversation derives from the Latin for 'turn around'. It is perhaps not surprising that, as Wolfe (2003) describes:

> through conversation we turn around our ideas and experiences with each other ... and we thereby also review those ideas and experiences ... conversation provides us with one way in which either to revisit our experience or to entertain possibilities of future experiences.

Closely linked to active listening is the gift of attending. As Weil writes:

> Those who are unhappy have no need for anything in this world but people capable of giving them their attention. The capacity to give one's attention to a sufferer is a very rare and difficult thing; it is almost a

miracle; it *is* a miracle. Nearly all those who think they have this capacity do not possess it. Warmth of heart, impulsiveness, pity are not enough.

(Weil, 2009)

The way that we look upon someone else is one of those almost imperceptible signals that can be the making or breaking of an encounter. Ruskin famously said, 'to be taught to see is to gain word and thought at once, and both true' (Birch, 2004). Chaplains are in many ways akin to artists in their practice. Like the artist, the chaplain is called to give attention to familiar situations, to see beyond them or see them differently and to engage more deeply with the humanity and spirituality within them. Writing about looking at visual artefacts, Pattison (2007) argues that we need to rediscover what he terms 'haptic vision' – a way of looking that is richer, more nuanced, deeper, and that leads to a more intimate loving gaze. There is much in his argument for a chaplain to appropriate.

Trained in pastoral theology

If chaplains only need be good listeners, with the gift of attending, why not just employ counsellors or social workers? Stanworth (2004) gives one answer to that question when she comments: 'It is hard to see how I can accompany anyone facing deep questions of meaning and identity without some prior contemplation of my own personhood.' To help those they encounter explore their spiritual story, chaplains need to develop the capacity for systematic theological reflection on lived experience that comes from training in pastoral theology. This can be seen in the person specifications for various chaplaincy jobs. A prison chaplain advertisement, for example, requires the applicant 'to have received training to a recognized academic competence in theology, biblical studies, and pastoral care'. Similarly alongside a degree or equivalent, a university chaplaincy post requires 'previous experience in a pastoral role'. While this book concentrates on chaplaincy from a Christian perspective it is noticeable that across the faith spectrum there is a requirement to combine pastoral and theological expertise. Alongside training in the Holy Qur'an and Islamic Law, a specification for a Muslim hospital chaplain required three years' employment in a community role or pastoral-care position.

In combining such training and experience the role of the chaplain is not to tell people what to think but rather to help them explore and think for themselves. As Lance Blake (Chapter 12) notes in relation to his work in a hospice, for answers to be authentic and useful we must own them ourselves. Williams (1999) illustrates this point using a passage from *Winnie-the-Pooh*. Pooh is tracking paw marks in the snow around a spinney. Joined by Piglet, they become increasingly alarmed as the number of paw marks increases, until Christopher Robin intervenes. From up a tree he observes how they were just about to go round the spinney for a fourth time (Milne, 1926). Williams suggests that Christopher Robin was able to help Pooh to new insight because he was in a different position from him and therefore could see something not visible to Pooh. From his vantage point Christopher Robin was able to share 'what he saw – not as judgement, but as information that could be shared for the other to reflect upon; not as "I know it better than you" but as "I know it differently from you and perhaps that could be useful to you"'.

Chaplains often minister in secular organizations to those who predominantly do not belong to and/or believe in a particular faith tradition. As some chaplains note in the earlier parts of this book, this has led to frustrations in having to battle against a secularist thread and a questioning of the place of religion within such an institution. It is certainly true that there has been a sharp decline in church attendance over the past decades. However, drawing on Taylor's work *A Secular Age* and his own experience as a hospital chaplain, Swift (2009) argues that it is a mistake to equate this with 'the demise of religious longings and spiritual desire'. King et al. (2006), when looking at measuring people's spiritual beliefs, noted that 'people with no religious affiliation find it difficult to express their spiritual beliefs and experiences'. Accordingly decline in orthodox religious expression, far from removing the need for chaplains, may actually generate a need for chaplains who, as skilful interpreters, 'listen openly, and respond creatively, to personal spiritualities' (Swift, 2009).

Skilled in handling liturgy and liturgically based ritual

Alongside providing pastoral care nearly all job descriptions for chaplaincy posts mention the leading of worship. In the stories gathered here this ranges from a small Communion with more apologies for absence than attendants to a large memorial service for a whole institution; from the cold horror of repatriating a dead airman from Afghanistan to the warmth and intimacy of a candlelit prayer meeting. Chaplains clearly need to be confident in leading public worship in a variety of situations. However, as well as leading they need to be competent in creating fitting liturgy and ritual. In early 2010 the *Doonesbury* comic strip (Trudeau, 2010) written by Garry Trudeau introduced a new character: a female Army chaplain. In one strip, having been called to the hospital the chaplain is grateful to discover that the soldier will recover. However, having given the good news the medic continues by saying that the soldier was worried he would not be eligible for rites as he is from a multi-faith family. The chaplain answers that something could have been sorted out. Amazed, the medic asks, 'You do mash-ups?' to which the chaplain responds, 'It's not pretty, but yeah.' Although the context might be different such a scene would, one suspects, resonate with many chaplains. Bill Burleigh, for example, writing about children's funerals (Chapter 13), states the need for 'huge flexibility' and combining 'balloons, poems and "fairy dust"' with a 'gently worded prayer of commendation'. While in some situations there may be fitting ready-made liturgy, in others there simply is no liturgy and/or ritual that can be applied direct from a prayer book. Accordingly chaplains need to be comfortable with designing liturgy and ritual to suit different situations. Writing in relation to hospital chaplains, Swift (2006) makes the point that others do not have 'this ability to handle ancient words (and invent a few new ones on occasions!)'. This unique capacity provides another argument for not replacing chaplains with other professionals.

If, as this chapter seeks to suggest, much of the work of chaplains is about helping people through times of transition, then it is perhaps unsurprising that liturgy and ritual are important. Writing from an anthropological perspective, Jenkins (2006), himself a former chaplain, suggests that one of the features of ritual is that it is 'often to do with transition'. The use of rituals in helping people through difficult times is well attested. Hodge (2001), for example, notes how rituals 'serve to ease anxiety and dread, alleviate isolation, promote a sense of security, and establish a sense of being loved and appreciated'. Although not central to the concerns of this chapter, it is worth pausing here to consider what might be going on when ritual is performed. Rappaport (1999), in his majestic *Ritual and Religion in the Making of Humanity*, argues that ritual is a form of communication. He contends that 'ritual is not simply an alternative way to express any manner of thing, but that certain meanings and effects can best, or even *only*, be expressed or achieved in ritual'. He continues by stating that while the boundary is not sharp or clear, ritual's efficacy may be understood as physical, through the deployment of matter and energy, or meaningful, grounded in principles of communication. This idea that ritual – and we might add liturgy – helps us communicate meaning in situations where we struggle to find the right words is supported by writing from a religious perspective. Macquarrie (1997), for example, states that we live in a sacramental universe where the material world 'can become a door or channel of communication, through which he [God] comes to us and we may go to him'. In other words, in the pastoral context ritual and liturgy offer a way for people to honour the different and sometimes paradoxical things they implicitly feel at a deep level, and for their searching and struggling to be expressed, articulated and validated.

Critical, creative and reflexive thinkers

There is merit at this point in reflecting on a statement made by Orchard (2000) concerning different styles of chaplaincy encountered in her research into the work of hospital chaplains in London. Orchard describes in glowing terms what she calls an 'empty handed' approach encountered in one hospital that 'requires no expertise' on the part of the caregiver. It is certainly true that chaplains should not arrive with pre-prescribed solutions to pre-perceived problems. In this way the chaplain must indeed come empty handed. However, in the light of all the above it is difficult to agree with the claim that 'no expertise' is needed. Likewise Swift (2006) is correct to challenge Orchard's assertion that anyone can go in empty handed. In any pastoral situation our hands are full of unspoken signals – dress, titles, expectations – that cannot be put down and that influence the encounter. Chaplains are, as Swinton and Mowat (2006) state of researchers, co-creators not only of the mode and content of an encounter but also of the story that is told within it. For this reason chaplains need to be critically self-aware, developing the reflexivity to identify and reflect critically on the ways in which they may have shaped an encounter.

The term 'develop' is used purposefully here. With perhaps the best known being the Myers-Briggs Type Indicator, there are various personality indicators that can be used to measure psychological preferences in how people perceive the world and make decisions. In their work looking at the personality types of Anglican hospital chaplains, Francis et al. (2009) observe that they comprise a discrete group within the more general pool of Anglican clergy. He argues that their distinctive personality preferences make them particularly well suited to the pastoral work they carry out. There is, however, a potential problem here in relation to the decision-making preference: thinking or feeling. Dominant feelers are inclined to make decisions through empathy, considering 'what is important to them and to others involved'. By contrast, dominant thinkers prefer a more detached standpoint, looking 'at the logical consequences of a choice or action' (Myers, 2000). Only 3 per cent of hospital chaplains surveyed by Francis had thinking rather than feeling as their dominant preference. Consequently, Fraser (2010) argues that there should be a constructive and sustained effort to cultivate critical thinking and reflecting within chaplaincy so that it is not seen as the domain of the few dominant thinkers but a skill of chaplains across the board. Here it is important to point out that a preference for feeling should not be used as an excuse for a lack of critical thinking (or anything else). Although we tend to develop and nurture our preferred pattern of being and doing, many type indicators point out that we should learn to use our shadow side (that is, the opposites of our preferences) if we are to live in a balanced and holistic way.

The importance of developing reflexivity and having critical reflect-ive skills can be seen in the course content of several postgraduate chaplaincy courses. For example, St Mary's University College, Twickenham, offers a number of postgraduate chaplaincy courses that aim among other things to 'develop the reflective skills necessary for sustained and fruitful engagement in chaplaincy work'. Probably the most developed chaplaincy course is the Master of Theology in Chaplaincy Studies (MThC) offered by St Michael's College in partnership with Cardiff University School of Religious and Theological Studies. One of the aims of the MThC is to 'improve the intellectual, reflective and practical competence', with the related outcome to develop the 'critical reflective skills that will enable you the better to respond to the pressures of your professional activities'.

Critical thinking and reflecting are important for a number of reasons. In the stories here, for many people the point of engagement with chaplaincy is occasioned by a crisis. In her work as a university chaplain, Clare McBeath describes (Chapter 6) dealing with deaths and serious illnesses, child protection and mental-health issues, suspected pregnancies and domestic abuse, as well as concerns around bereavement, sexuality, accommodation, the criminal justice system, finance, drugs/alcohol, asylum applications and forced marriages. In such situations chaplains must be able to reflect thoughtfully upon the issues raised if they are to help people attempt to make sense of what has happened to them and all they are going through. As Stephen Robbins states of Army chaplains (Chapter 2), 'easy theology' does not work in this environment. Indeed even without the crises, the context of a chaplain's work will often raise such complex theological issues as suffering and healing, justice and forgiveness, pacifism and just war. The imagination of chaplains in responding to human need is acknowledged by Cobb (2007). He is critical, though, of how often ingenuity is justified on pastoral rather than theological grounds, and reminds chaplains of the importance of remaining 'alert to the theological task of self-conscious critical thinking, inquiry and interpretation'.

As well as being important in supporting those they attend, critical thinking and sustained reflection are also vital for a chaplain's own well-being. Dawn Colley (Chapter 17) writes of prison chaplaincy that this 'comes with a hazard warning'; and Bill Burleigh describes the 'hurt that sometimes seems slowly to sap energy, even faith' in connection with working in a children's hospital. Exhaustion and burnout are all too often associated with those in caring professions, where attending to the needs of others can often mean containing our own needs. Some of these issues are explored in a wonderful episode of *The Simpsons* entitled 'In Marge We Trust' (Dean and Donik, 1997). Having become concerned about Reverend Lovejoy's lack of enthusiasm about helping people, Marge begins working for the church as 'The Listen Lady'. At first things go well and Marge has soon replaced Reverend Lovejoy as the source of help for Springfield's troubled. However, when attempting to support Ned Flanders, Marge soon finds that she has got in beyond her depth. Turning in desperation to Reverend Lovejoy, she cries out, 'Where do the helpers turn when they need help?'

Clearly context plays some part in affecting our stress levels but our own actions are likely to be a sizeable factor as well. Ministering to a whole organization or institution, chaplains may frequently feel guilty that they have not done enough. Jane Speck (Chapter 10) notes how easy it is 'to end up living with a permanent sense of unspecified failure'. In terms of effectiveness there is a point at which if we take on more we simply become increasingly ineffective. A piece of advice that has stuck with me over the years is the simple saying, 'If you never say no, of what value is your yes?' One contributor to this book describes leaving chaplaincy due to an awareness of potential burnout. Chaplains need to be aware of how they are coping with the emotional and spiritual demands of their jobs. They should seek both to develop a strong prayer life and to put support structures in place. This includes having a spiritual director and/or a work mentor/supervisor to reflect on spiritual and work life respectively. There is a real opportunity here for church hierarchies to take chaplaincy more seriously by helping chaplains find people with whom to carry out such critical reflection.

Given the context of continuous change in which many chaplains work, another area to be aware of is coping with unresolved or open endings. In an interesting article looking at endings in literature, Jack (2006) suggests that it is a human need to discover or create apposite endings 'so that the here and now is given a coherence it would otherwise lack'. She supports this by quoting from Barbara Herrnstein Smith's *Poetic Closure: A Study of How Poems End*:

> haunted, perhaps, by the spectre of that ultimate arbitrary conclusion, we take particular delight, not in all endings, but in those that are designed. Our most gratifying experiences tend to be not the interminable ones but rather those that conclude.

As several of our contributors note, chaplaincy is not always neat and tidy. It is quite likely that a chaplain may only accompany someone for a brief period of time and not know how the story continues. Writing in relation to clients who simply stop attending counselling sessions, Horton (2000) notes that 'incomplete endings by default can haunt therapists for some time'. This suggests that chaplains need to be aware of (subconscious) temptations to create artificially fitting endings. The feeling aroused by the lack of control over endings may be another area for chaplains to look at with spiritual directors or clinical supervisors.

Other supporting skills

This chapter has concentrated on the tools necessary to provide good pastoral care to the people whom chaplains encounter, alongside looking after their own well-being. While pastoral care is clearly central to the role of most chaplains, there are further skills that chaplains will need in order to carry out their work. It is important, for example, that chaplains can communicate with a wide range of people. Tim Bryan (Chapter 16) describes how he can go from attending the senior managers' meeting – an opportunity to understand and affect how things are done – to visiting vulnerable prisoners. In a similar way David Simpson (Chapter 3) writes of the naval chaplain being 'the friend and adviser of all on board'. Related to this, several chaplains write about the challenging but enriching environment of multi-faith working. Perhaps the most astonishing picture here is from Charles Thody (Chapter 15) recounting a Roman Catholic bishop and a Pagan Wiccan chaplain discussing a patient together. Clearly in such situations chaplains need to be able to engage critically while respecting views different from their own.

In addition chaplains with management accountability may have a whole raft of administrative tasks to undertake. Among other duties, Nigel Goodfellow (Chapter 14) lists responsibility for the department's budget, implementing strategy and service development and recording and monitoring chaplaincy activity. Clearly those who lead teams need to be able to coordinate and delegate as well as manage the development and review of those under them. Linked to this the support of volunteers is attested to by several chaplains. Accordingly chaplains at various levels would benefit from training in pastoral supervision. Finally, whether part of a team or not, chaplains may often end up working alone and need to be able to prioritize and manage their ongoing work. For some this task will be greater still. Jim Craig (Chapter 22) describes having to create his own job description and objectives from scratch. This is unfortunately suggestive of the marginality noted in the Introduction to this book. While it is right that chaplains are involved in writing job descriptions, in doing so they should not be left without support.

Conclusion

Standing on the Church/world interface, speaking to the world of God and to the Church of the world, chaplains in carrying out their work require a deep well of resources on which to draw. From a biblical perspective they need to be like 'the master of a household who brings out of his treasure what is new and what is old' (Matthew 13.52). A more modern and unorthodox model could come from the world of *Harry Potter* and the 'Room of Requirement' (Rowling, 2003). This is a magical room in Hogwarts School that is 'always equipped for the seeker's needs' and so might be said to contain everything and nothing. But far from relying on magic, being a chaplain is a challenging and demanding vocation requiring a high degree of expertise and proficiency.

Ranging from the contribution towards general well-being that comes from a ministry of presence to the provision of help and comfort to those in some sort of trouble, grief or distress, I have suggested that a key role of chaplains is the provision of pastoral care and the supporting of people through difficult times or times of transition. In attending, listening and building relationships of trust, chaplains use counselling skills such as empathy and unconditional positive regard. Importantly, though, chaplains need more skills than simply being good listeners. The offering of a spiritual perspective – exploring how the person is in relation to their beliefs about themselves and the world and seeking to explore sources of strength and hope – requires a grounding in pastoral theology. Alongside this, be it a simple prayer or something more extensive, chaplains also need to be able to use liturgy and ritual with creativity and imagination. Finally, often working in pressurized environments and dealing with the crises that arise from them requires chaplains to have a stability that comes from their own well of faith and the ability to think and reflect critically.

While the role of chaplains and the skills required can be remarkably similar despite sometimes radically differing contexts, context should not be forgotten. In Chapter 23, summarizing his case studies Andrew Todd suggests that in comparison to healthcare chaplaincy, military and prison chaplains have a greater institutional drive towards a coherent model of chaplaincy. In support of this, recent literature from both healthcare and higher education chaplaincy has noted a lack of clarity among chaplains as to their role or the range of models and practice that exists (Caring for the Spirit NHS Project, 2003; Clines, 2008). With increasing pressures upon chaplaincies to demonstrate their value, it seems likely that where there is not an institutional desire to shape chaplaincy, chaplains have adapted their practice to find niches in which to survive. In responding to such demands it would clearly be advantageous for there to be a greater collective understanding of role and purpose, not just within sectors but also, where possible, across sectors. One hope of this book is that in the sharing of stories, such a conversation is begun.

References

Birch, D. (ed.) (2004), *John Ruskin: Selected Writings*. Oxford: Oxford University Press.

Caring for the Spirit NHS Project (2003), 'Caring for the Spirit: A Strategy for the Chaplaincy and Spiritual Healthcare Workforce'. South Yorkshire Workforce Development Confederation, available at <www.nhs-chaplaincy-collaboratives. com/resources/caringforthespirit0311.pdf> [accessed September 2010].

Clines, J. M. S. (2008), *Faiths in Higher Education Chaplaincy*. London: Church of England Board of Education.

Cobb, M. (2007), 'Change and Challenge: The Dynamic of Chaplaincy'. *Scottish Journal of Healthcare Chaplaincy* 10/1, pp. 4–10.

Dean, S. D. and Donik, C. W. (1997), 'In Marge We Trust', *The Simpsons Heaven and Hell* [Video]. Los Angeles: Twentieth Century Fox.

Francis, L., Hancocks, G., Swift, C. and Robbins, M. (2009), 'Distinctive Call, Distinctive Profile: The Psychological Type Profile of Church of England Full-time Hospital Chaplains'. *Practical Theology* 2/2, pp. 269–84.

Fraser, D. (2010), 'Pastoral Heart and Critical Mind: The Shaping of Chaplaincy in the NHS'. *Practical Theology* 3/2, pp. 179–90.

Hodge, D. R. (2001), 'Spiritual Assessment: A Review of Major Qualitative Methods and a New Framework for Assessing Spirituality'. *Social Work* 46/3, pp. 203–14.

Horton, I. (2000), 'Structuring', in Feltham, C. and Horton, I. (eds), *Handbook of Counselling and Psychotherapy*. London: Sage.

Jack, A. (2006), 'The Intolerable Wrestle with Words and Meanings: John 21, T. S. Eliot and the Sense of an Ending'. *The Expository Times* 117/12, pp. 496–501.

Jenkins, T. (2006), *An Experiment in Providence*. London: SPCK.

King, M., Jones, L., Barnes, K., Low, J. and Walker, C. (2006), 'Measuring Spiritual Belief: Development and Standardization of a Beliefs and Values Scale'. *Psychological Medicine* 36/3, pp. 417–25.

Koenig, H. G. (2008), 'Concerns About Measuring "Spirituality" in Research'. *The Journal of Nervous and Mental Disease* 196/5, pp. 349–55.

Lyall, D. (2001), *Integrity of Pastoral Care*. London: SPCK.

Macquarrie, J. (1997), *A Guide to the Sacraments*. London: SCM Press.

Milne, A. A. (1926), *Winnie-the-Pooh*. London: Methuen (repr. 1965).

Myers, I. B. (2000), *Introduction to Type*, 6th edn. Oxford: Oxford Psychologists Press.

Newitt, M. (2010), 'The Role and Skills of a Hospital Chaplain: Reflections Based on a Case Study'. *Practical Theology* 3/2, pp. 163–77.

Orchard, H. (2000), *Hospital Chaplaincy: Modern, Dependable?* Sheffield: Sheffield Academic Press/Lincoln Theological Institute.

Pattison, S. (2007), *Seeing Things*. London: SCM Press.

Rappaport, R. A. (1999), *Ritual and Religion in the Making of Humanity*. Cambridge: Cambridge University Press.

Rowling, J. K. (2003), *Harry Potter and the Order of the Phoenix*. London: Bloomsbury.

Smith, B. H. (1968), *Poetic Closure: A Study of How Poems End*. Chicago: University of Chicago Press.

Stanworth, R. (2004), *Recognising Spiritual Needs in People who are Dying*. Oxford: Oxford University Press.

Swift, C. (2006), 'The Function of the Chaplain in the Government of the Sick in English Acute Hospitals'. PhD thesis, University of Sheffield, Sheffield Centre for Health and Related Research.

Swift, C. (2009), *Hospital Chaplaincy in the Twenty-first Century: The Crisis of Spiritual Care on the NHS*. Farnham: Ashgate.

Swinton, J. and Mowat, H. (2006), *Practical Theology and Qualitative Research*. London: SCM Press.

Taylor, C. (2007), *A Secular Age*. Cambridge, MA/London: Belknap.

Trudeau, G. (2010), *Doonesbury* [Cartoon], available at <www.gocomics.com/doonesbury/2010/05/18> [accessed September 2010].

Weil, S. (2009), *Waiting for God*. New York: Harper Perennial Modern Classics.

Williams, S. (1999), 'The Therapist as Outsider: The Truth of the Stranger'. *British Journal of Psychotherapy* 16/1, pp. 3–15.

Wolfe, M. (2003), 'Conversation', in Richardson, L. D. and Wolfe, M. (eds), *Principles and Practice of Informal Education*. Oxford: Routledge Falmer.

25

Exploring models of chaplaincy

MIRANDA THRELFALL-HOLMES

In discussing the different models of chaplaincy with which we work it is important to be clear that there is no one 'correct' model. Chaplains are likely to work with different models at different times and will probably identify with aspects of all or many of those suggested in this chapter. Models are inevitably artificial. However, identifying and discussing specific models can be extremely helpful in two particular ways. First, it is a helpful aid to reflection on what chaplaincy is and what it is for, providing a framework for that reflection. This will be particularly useful both for those who are already chaplains and who seek to reflect on their work, and those who may be considering entering chaplaincy. Second, thinking about models also helps to place chaplaincy within more general discussions of ministry. Chaplaincy is not fundamentally different in kind from other types of ministry. Chaplains, as well as those who minister in parish situations and pioneer ministers of various kinds, model Christian leadership and engage in Christian ministry in ways that are shaped to a greater or lesser extent by their contexts. The discussion of models presented here will no doubt resonate strongly with the experience of ministers in a wide variety of contexts, and it is hoped that it will prove a useful aid to reflection on ministry for all.

The most notable difference in the ministry contexts of chaplains and other clergy or ministers is the nature of their 'employer'. While some chaplains are partially or wholly funded by the churches or combine a part-time chaplaincy role with parochial or other ministry, many are employed by the institution in which they work. This chapter looks in particular at the models for chaplaincy that such employers hold, alongside the more conventional theological models with which clergy are more familiar. Taking a closer look at the models of chaplaincy that you and your employer, or others around you, are working with can be helpful in explaining or analysing many of the conflicts that arise in chaplaincy. That is not to say that understanding models will, like a magic bullet, suddenly solve all the issues and tensions that a chaplain faces! However, laying out and considering different models can help to depersonalize issues and tensions, putting them into both proper perspective and an explanatory framework. Often such tensions may result from mismatches between the expectations and models of chaplaincy being used, consciously or often unconsciously, by both the chaplain and others around them.

There are numerous models of ministry in the extensive literature on ministry and vocation. For example, Greenwood (1994) presents a Trinitarian model while Croft (1999) uses the historic threefold orders of the Church to model key aspects of ministry today. Not everyone finds such overarching models helpful. Other writing on ministry offers exhaustive (and often exhausting!) lists of desirable attributes and aspects of the role. This ranges from the classic though rather dated *The Christian Priest Today* (Ramsey, 1972) to Pritchard's more modern though similarly daunting *The Life and Work of a Priest* (2007). Historically George Herbert's seventeenth-century *The Country Parson* – widely available in a variety of modern editions – has been extremely influential in forming many of our assumptions about what ministry, especially parish ministry, should be. Both Percy in *Clergy: The Origin of Species* (2006) and Billings in *Making God Possible* (2010) make the important point that cultural context is critical both in the models that emerge and in determining the best model for particular times, places or tasks.

A variety of models of chaplaincy are presented and discussed in the existing literature. Examples can be found in various essays in *Chaplaincy: The Church's Sector Ministries* (Legood, 1999). Likewise Robinson (2004) gives a useful overview of a range of models that have been applied to chaplaincy (not simply relating to university chaplaincy) in *Ministry Among Students*. The models and metaphors he quotes for chaplaincy or for individual aspects of the chaplain's role range from therapist to jester! But there is a notable gap in the literature. The majority of writing and reflection on chaplaincy has been almost entirely from the perspective of either the chaplains themselves or the churches. Little attention has been paid to the viewpoint of the other major party in the equation, namely the institutions receiving or employing the chaplains and what they want or expect. One exception is Orchard's (2000) study of healthcare chaplaincy, which helpfully distinguishes between models that are primarily characterized by 'sponsor defined' (church) or 'employer defined' parameters. If we as chaplains think we are doing one thing, while our employers think we are here to do something else, the scene is set for disputes and misunderstandings.

So I will structure this discussion under two main subheadings. First, theological models – those held by chaplains themselves or more widely by the Church: What do we think we are doing? Second, secular models – those held by others, by those receiving, employing or accessing chaplaincy: What do they think chaplains are for? I have drawn widely on the contributions included in this book, personal conversations with both other chaplains and representatives of employing institutions, and on material from those institutions, such as job descriptions, as well as on the published literature on ministry. However, the synthesis and categorization presented here represents my own judgement and opinion; it should be noted that the individuals and institutions on whose views I have drawn would not necessarily use this terminology.

Theological models include:

- the missionary
- the pastor
- the incarnational or sacramental
- the historical-parish model
- a cluster of models centring on being an agent of challenge or change, such as prophet, jester, social activist.

Secular models include:

- the provider of pastoral care
- the spiritual carer
- the diversity model
- the tradition/heritage model
- a 'meta-model' that summarizes many of these – the specialist service provider.

It will already be clear that these sets of models, and the models within, are neither mutually exclusive nor incompatible. Many, probably most chaplains will hold at least one or two of the theological models simultaneously and acknowledge that aspects of some or all of the others are important to them. Nevertheless it can be a useful exercise to decide in what order they are important in your own ministry or your own conceptions of chaplaincy; and in what order you think they are important to your own employing institution or sector. Would you choose the same set of metaphors or models when speaking of your ministry as a chaplain to other clergy, and to a review of chaplaincy services in your institution? Alternatively are there images or models that are important to you that you would consciously avoid choosing in such discussions?

Theological models

The missionary model

At heart many chaplains see their vocation in terms analogous to being a missionary. They have been called or sent to a particular place, largely unchurched. Their task is to bring the gospel to the people there in whatever ways may suit the context. This model often underlies the enthusiasm many chaplains feel for their work and the deep pull towards chaplaincy they describe, as for example in the contributions here from Ruth Hake, John Boyers and Jim Craig (Chapters 1, 21, 22). A large part of the attraction is that it offers the opportunity to: 'do what we were really ordained for'; work in the mission field of contemporary society; proclaim the gospel unencumbered by the need to maintain crumbling church buildings; reach those traditionally unreached by the churches.

Because the needs of people and means of communicating the gospel vary widely between different contexts, there is no one typical pattern of ministry for those who see their ministry primarily in this way. This is a model that tends to provide the motivation for the chaplain's ministry rather than a specific programme or direction. In various contexts the chaplain may, for example, need to focus on proclaiming God's love and redemption primarily through providing pastoral care, seeking to reform structures or through his or her own presence and being. When the context changes, whether through the chaplain moving or a change within the organization, the way in which the mission is expressed may also need to change. A need to change the modus operandi may be a significant source of stress if a chaplain has a strong affinity for a particular way of working.

This model can be particularly feared by employers, for whom 'mission' may well be a dirty word. The implications are all too often perceived to be intolerance, exclusivism and the denunciation of those who do not convert. However, the missionary model should in fact be inherently respectful of and responsive to the context in which it is situated. Bosch (1991) argues that from the beginning the missionary message of the Church incarnated itself in the life and world of those around it; it is therefore inherently contextual and continually to be renewed and reconceived. The context and thus range of expressions of mission will be at least in part formed by the expectations of the employing institution, including respect for values such as diversity, equal opportunities and tolerance. These expectations are likely to be expressed in the chaplain's job description or service-level agreement, or in more generic strategy and policy statements. Those who become chaplains to share the love of God with people in hard-to-reach places need to be particularly skilled at the task of discerning the best means and tools of mission in a particular context. The missionary model is probably the hardest to attempt to communicate to those outside the Church, which raises issues of terminology and language that are explored in more detail in Chapter 26.

The pastor model

On this understanding the role of the chaplain is primarily to care for people. The task of ministry is seen primarily as one of sharing in God's love for and care for all people, unconditionally and without demanding any response. The chaplain may explicitly identify this role with the example of Jesus' self-giving and sacrificial love for all.

There is a wide variety of genres or metaphors within the pastoral-care model, and any combination of these may be held. For example, chaplains with this view of their role may think of themselves primarily as a friendly listening ear, a companion on the journey of life, a 'Samaritan' or a therapist or counsellor (and may seek professional training in these areas). The traditional priestly image of the 'Father' may be integrated within this model if a chaplain sees him- (or possibly her-) self in a quasi-parental role of advice and support.

In contrast with the missionary model, this is often the easiest to explain to those outside the Church. However, it is vulnerable where it fails to be distinctive. As Mark Newitt points out in Chapter 24, chaplains need to be more than just good listeners. If an employing institution has other providers of similar types of care, such as counsellors or mentors, then chaplaincy may be perceived as duplicating what is on offer elsewhere and not adding value in a distinctive and/or cost-effective way. Chaplains working on this model may find that they need to gain additional qualifications in counselling or related skills in order to be seen as credible providers of pastoral care in an increasingly professionalized market.

The incarnational or sacramental model

This model, like the previous one, is often rooted theologically in the imitation of Christ but is primarily inspired by the being and nature of Jesus rather than his actions. Chaplains taking this model as their inspiration will often speak of their ministry being essentially 'incarnational'. They see their primary role as embodying something of God in the places where they minister. Examples in this volume include the contributions by Ruth Hake, Anna de Lange and Dana Delap (Chapters 1, 4, 18). Others, such as David Simpson (Chapter 3), prefer to use the language of sacrament to express a similar idea. Here the chaplain is understood as a 'walking sacrament'. The stuff of everyday life is taken and used to convey the reality and love of God.

Where this is the guiding model of chaplaincy, ministry will often be spoken of in terms of 'a ministry of presence' or 'being not doing'. There is a strong familial connection between this model of chaplaincy and ontological theories of ordination. Being a chaplain, being a minister or priest, is something that one essentially is rather than does. The assumption is that God will work in and through the presence of the chaplain.

While this can be a very powerful model for those within the community of faith, it will be immediately clear that it presents a problem in communication with those outside the Church, especially those with no faith commitment. Without a belief in the God who will do the work, this model sounds suspiciously as if it is offering a chaplain who will do nothing except (perhaps) wear a dog collar and wander around looking religious! It does, however, have considerable overlap with the next model, which may offer a better way of communicating the strengths of this approach.

The historical-parish model

Some chaplains and even some employers speak of chaplaincy in terms of parish ministry. A recent recruitment advertisement for Army chaplains had the words 'this is my parish' superimposed on a picture of a war zone. Within the Anglican tradition the parish model of ministry relates to a specific locality. Until the industrial revolution this would be the place where most parishioners spent their working and domestic lives. A parish priest was thus physically present among and potentially involved in the whole of life. By contrast, in contemporary society, with many people commuting to work, the parish is no longer the centre of all aspects of life. Some chaplaincy appointments, such as industrial and workplace chaplaincies, attempt to address this division.

For many chaplains the historical-parish model describes very closely the context in which they work. In an academic context, particularly in one of the older universities or a boarding school, the college or school may well be both the home and workplace of the students and some of the staff. Likewise in the armed forces, particularly when on deployment, there is a strong link between work and residence. In other contexts, such as prisons or hospitals, there may be aspects of this model, particularly where people are there for longer periods.

Where the parish model is relevant, chaplaincy may have a particular focus on simply being present in and engaged with the whole life of the place. Here there is significant overlap with the sacramental model. Presence around the place opens up opportunities for conversations; for the sharing of dilemmas; for informal confessions; for interested people to make tentative enquiries about Christian faith. Presence is not important simply functionally, as a way of enabling such encounters to happen. On this model, presence may be the theological essence of chaplaincy. From the perspective of those outside the Church, the parish model is often a very acceptable way to speak of a ministry of presence or the sacramental and incarnational ideas discussed above. The presence of a chaplain is often experienced – and valued – by those receiving such ministry as the Church validating their experiences, lives and work. One difficulty it can raise is that of time and resources. A vision of ministry to all will only rarely be a practical possibility. A profound sense of failure can result from the shortfall between the ideal and the reality on this model.

The prophetic or challenging models

There exists a whole cluster of models and metaphors for chaplaincy that have in common the theme of challenging the status quo and speaking prophetically into unjust or ungodly structures. The image of prophet is perhaps most commonly used. Other images include the jester and the political or social activist. Most chaplains would feel uncomfortable without some element of this aspect of ministry in their self-understanding. Many are particularly skilled at listening and discernment. It is often the case that chaplains hear what is really going on from many different sources, as Stephen Fagbemi points out (Chapter 7). They may well be able to bring insightful analysis to bear on the structures and policies of the organization of which they are part. But there are few institutions or organizations self-confident enough in their openness to scrutiny and committed enough to continual self-examination to choose to appoint – or welcome the appointment of – a court jester. Nor are organizations that decide they do need critique likely to turn to a chaplain for it – they are much more likely to call in the consultants.

This means that chaplains for whom the prophetic model is important may spend time feeling frustrated and marginalized. Whistle-blowing of abuses, while uncomfortable, may be relatively straightforward as procedures are likely to be in place. But there may be no obvious or easy way for chaplains to raise more general concerns about strategy or vision, make formal observations, such as that staff morale is suffering from a particular policy, or offer constructive suggestions for improvements.

Secular models

Already it will be clear that some of the language used by chaplains in reflecting upon their roles is very different from the language used by most employing institutions in describing the role of chaplain. Secular models of chaplaincy can be gleaned from official policy documents, reviews and job descriptions, though for any individual chaplain the task of discernment will go beyond these. They will want to discover, if possible, what are their senior management's and line managers' underlying attitudes to and assumptions about chaplaincy. These may be influenced by, for example, professional training or academic interests, childhood or adult experiences of Church, denominational background and of course personal experiences of clergy and chaplains, positive or negative. Nevertheless four distinct models of what some of the major employers of chaplains are looking for when they appoint a chaplain can be outlined.

The pastoral-care model

Here the chaplain is primarily seen as 'professional nice guy'. He or she is needed and valued mainly for the pastoral care given at times of crisis, whether for the community as a whole (such as the sudden death of a member of the community) or for individuals (examples commonly given are bereavement, depression and family crises). The chaplain's role is essentially one of damage limitation: he or she intervenes in such situations to prevent them developing into further, deeper crises more disruptive to the life of the institution.

The bottom-line value to the institution of chaplaincy provision on this model is that it contributes to the general well-being of people, both 'clients' and staff. The hope is that the provision of pastoral care will limit the disrupting and financially costly effects of crises on such indicators as staff absence (including time off with depression and stress-related illnesses), resignations, lower productivity, disruptive behaviour and – in relation to private schools and universities – withdrawal or dropout of fee-paying students. There are also more intangible benefits, which will often nonetheless be clearly articulated. For example, a school or university may anticipate that the provision of high-quality pastoral care will have a positive effect on the recruitment of students. Similar concerns may also affect other institutions bidding for government or agency funding, while a wide range of institutions and employers may hope that demonstrating, through the provision of chaplaincy, that they are a caring employer will have a positive impact on the recruitment and retention of good staff.

The spiritual-care model

On this understanding, typical of NHS documents, the spiritual health of individuals is seen as an important part of their overall health and well-being. Chaplains are appointed to meet spiritual and religious needs as part of the duty of care offered by the employing organization. They may be understood as experts skilled in the delivery of spiritual care, able to assess need and create care plans to meet that need. Where chaplains are well integrated into multi-disciplinary teamworking this may well be the case; rhetoric does not always match practice, however. Nigel Goodfellow (Chapter 14) describes how the chaplaincy role is often stereotyped as just to do with death and dying and/or organized religion. As with the pastoral model, with which there tends to be considerable overlap, the value of chaplaincy in this model is perceived to be its contribution to the holistic care principally of clients but sometimes also staff. This model tends to be more commonly held to where the health and well-being of those for whom the organization is responsible are felt to be its particular responsibility – primarily in hospitals and also to some extent in schools and prisons. In other contexts elements of this model may exist but tend to be integrated within the pastoral-care model.

The diversity model

Part of being seen to be a responsible employer these days lies in valuing and promoting diversity. Positively, having a diverse workforce is widely believed to stimulate creativity and productivity and thus directly impact economic or other indicators of success. A more negative stimulus is the need to be seen to be doing the right thing to guard against accusations of discrimination. In parallel with anti-discrimination legislation, diversity has been continually widened from its original remit (gender and colour) and is now generally understood to embrace people with a broad range of (dis)abilities and sexualities. Most importantly for our purposes, issues of colour or ethnicity have been broadened out substantially in recent years to include faith and culture.

The complexities and ambiguities surrounding diversity are discussed in greater depth by Andrew Todd in Chapter 23. It will suffice to say here that organizations have become increasingly aware of a need for good-quality advice in these areas, in which they often feel extremely vulnerable. They may be motivated both by fear of litigation (what adjustments to lecture times or meal arrangements might a university reasonably be expected to make in Ramadan, for example?) and by a desire to market themselves as responsible, modern employers. The main value of the chaplain to the institution will lie in providing professional advice and in demonstrating by virtue of the appointment that the organization has fulfilled its responsibilities in this area.

The tradition/heritage model

In some institutions, such as traditional colleges within universities, public schools and, as Andrew Todd's case study on Army chaplaincy describes, the military, chaplaincy provision may be seen as valuable precisely because it is part of the tradition or heritage of the institution. This is rarely explicitly articulated, however. In chaplaincy on this model the maintenance of the tradition will be given a high value. The chaplain will almost certainly be expected to provide 'civic' services on occasions such as Remembrance Sunday or on the anniversary of the founding of the institution, and to ensure that worship in the accepted tradition is maintained and done well. He or she might be expected not to rock the theological boat – though the tradition at some academic institutions may be that they should do precisely that!

The strength of this model should not be underestimated, though it is vulnerable to radical changes of direction following changes of corporate vision or simply of personnel at the head of an institution. The value of chaplaincy to the institution on this model lies primarily in adding distinction and distinctiveness to the image of the institution for marketing and recruitment purposes. Less tangibly the presence of chaplaincy on this model also contributes to and bolsters the self-understanding and sense of importance of the institution and individuals within it.

Secular meta-model: specialist service-provider

Most of the secular models can be held together loosely under the single umbrella understanding of the chaplain as a provider of specialist support services. From the point of view of the employing institution, the chaplain is there to provide certain professional services, whether as a pastoral carer, a spiritual carer, an expert in faith and faiths or as an expert practitioner and guardian of a cultural tradition. Chaplaincy is one resource among many within the range of support services provided by the institution, which may also include, for example, a counselling service, family liaison services or advice centres dealing with issues such as finances, accommodation or immigration. It is there, in most cases, on a 'take it or leave it' basis, to be accessed by those who want it or particularly need it.

Individuals in distress or in need of the particular professional competencies seen as being offered by chaplains – which may include bereavement support, faith-specific guidance on a moral issue or rituals – may be 'signposted' to the chaplaincy from other professional support services. The expectation is that the chaplain will, in turn, signpost those who need other specific services to the relevant place. While in common with other professional support services, chaplains are expected to be proactive and engaged with the community, the predominant assumption is that they are a service to be accessed by clients as needed. This is essentially a passive, consumer demand-led view of chaplaincy. This need not imply any denigration of the importance of chaplaincy, but from the institution's point of view reflects an emphasis on client choice and autonomy. It is for clients to decide to what extent they wish to access chaplaincy support services, unless they are particularly vulnerable or distressed, in which case another professional may make the judgement that a referral is in a person's best interest. At the heart of this model is a view of chaplaincy that sees it as primarily about spiritual/religious need, a view of belief that sees it as an individual choice and a view of the world that places a high value on individual freedom of choice.

Conclusion

It is interesting to reflect on how such secular models of chaplaincy might shed light on the way in which society as a whole views the ministry of the Church. It may well be the case that many of those who encounter parish clergy through, for example, the occasional offices, special school or community celebrations or at times of particular crisis, hold a similar view of the clergy as 'specialist service providers'. Such a view of what the Church is for may well clash with the theological models of ministry in which clergy are trained and that often underpin our self-understanding and sense of vocation. The experience of chaplains as analysed in this chapter may, it is hoped, be a useful contribution to understanding the different models of and assumptions about ministry held by those in and those outside the culture of the churches.

References

Billings, A. (2010), *Making God Possible*. London: SPCK.

Bosch, D. J. (1991), *Transforming Mission*. New York: Orbis.

Croft, S. (1999), *Ministry in Three Dimensions*. London: Darton, Longman & Todd.

Greenwood, R. (1994), *Transforming Priesthood*. London: SPCK.

Legood, G. (ed.) (1999), *Chaplaincy: The Church's Sector Ministries*. London: Cassell.

Orchard, H. (2000), *Hospital Chaplaincy: Modern, Dependable?* Sheffield: Sheffield Academic Press/Lincoln Theological Institute.

Percy, M. (2006), *Clergy: The Origin of Species*. London: Continuum.

Pritchard, J. (2007), *The Life and Work of a Priest*. London: SPCK.

Ramsey, M. (1972), *The Christian Priest Today*. London: SPCK.

Robinson, S. (2004), *Ministry Among Students*. Norwich: Canterbury Press.

26

Values and tensions

MIRANDA THRELFALL-HOLMES

As identified in Chapter 25, tensions can arise out of the different models of chaplaincy held by chaplains themselves and the institutions in which they minister. Other tensions may arise where the values of the institution clash with the values of the chaplain or his or her sponsoring church or faith community. At still other times such tensions can arise not from actual clashes of values but from perceptions or assumptions about what the values of the other might be. In the context of a general unease about the role of religion in public life, for example, conflict can arise between the perceived faith agenda of the chaplain (often assumed to be overtly evangelistic) and the avowedly and determinedly secular or non-partisan agenda of the employing institution. It is worth noting, though, that this is almost entirely experienced by chaplains as a clash of perceptions arising from the institution's misconception of what a chaplain's mission is. Rarely if ever do chaplains report that they have found their *actual* agenda or mission clashing with the interests of the institution, although the latter's fear of such a clash can itself be problematic.

This chapter suggests various strategies for identifying the values of an institution and bringing alternative values into constructive dialogue with them. It also highlights some of the key areas that can be the focus of tensions in the work of chaplains. As in the previous chapter, a deliberate attempt is made to see things from the point of view of the organizations that employ chaplains as well as from the perspectives of the chaplains themselves, and to use non-theological language wherever possible to aid conversation between these differing standpoints.

Identifying institutional values

Chaplaincy almost always takes place within an institution that self-identifies as 'secular', the most common exceptions being some schools and colleges with explicit faith foundations. But secular does not mean value-free. In many cases the self-description 'secular' is used precisely to make the point that one of the values of the institution is equality and diversity or equal respect for all regardless of creed. The term may be used to exclude faith-based value systems explicitly from the decision-making processes of the institution, but more commonly it is intended to signal that all (or at least multiple) value systems are treated as equally valid and/or worthy of respect.

The values of individual institutions will vary greatly. Nevertheless it is possible to identify certain values that are widely held by contemporary secular institutions and organizations. These can be derived from mission statements, statements of corporate values and the areas organizations choose to emphasize in staff-training modules. Such a list, from which at least some are likely to be held by any given institution, includes:

- excellence in the relevant field of expertise
- equality/fairness of access to the services provided
- respect for all, with particular regard to non-discrimination according to race, gender, sexuality/gender reassignment, religion, age, (dis)ability and so on
- efficiency/providing value for money
- transparency/honesty/accountability
- profitability/shareholder value
- being a good 'corporate citizen'/community engagement
- being a caring, responsible employer
- environmental awareness/low environmental impact.

These are all good and honest values for an organization to have and it is important to recognize that where they clash with, or cause tensions with, faith-based values, we cannot simply assume that faith-based values will or should triumph. For example, in recent years the 'business case' for chaplaincy has been called into question by several NHS Trusts. In response to financial pressures, even the Church of England has contemplated cutting posts such as the National Adviser for Higher Education. In such an environment it is unsurprising that a secular institution may call into question whether chaplaincy can or should be funded, and on what grounds. It is a reasonable question to ask. Chaplaincy may be central to the provision of one value of the institution, such as to provide holistically for those in its care, but the imperative to deliver value for money may be equally strong. And especially when an institution is publicly funded, delivering value for money can itself be an ethical value as well as a business need. However personally threatened chaplains may feel by the asking of such a question, however tempting it may be to see it as further evidence of the marginalization of religion, we must recognize that at a time of budgetary pressures and threatened redundancies in all departments it would be irresponsible not to ask it. It is essential that chaplains avoid falling into the trap of seeing themselves as one interest group among many but rather that they maintain a sense of perspective about their work and the overall work of the institution. As Pattison (2000) states, 'If pastors have no perspective on their work they risk complacency, stagnation and possible complicity with that that is less than good or desirable.'

The core values of an institution, or at least the ones of which the institution is most proud, will almost always be prominently displayed on literature and/or websites in the form of a mission statement or similar. This will normally summarize what the organization exists for, as well as the key values that will guide it in pursuit of its aim(s). Here, for example, is the statement of purpose of the UK Prison Service: 'Her Majesty's Prison Service serves the public by keeping in custody those committed by the courts. Its duty is to look after them with humanity and help them lead law-abiding and useful lives in custody and after release' (HM Prison Service, 2004).

The NHS has a constitution that sets out seven key principles, including that the services it provides are 'available to all irrespective of gender, race, disability, age, sexual orientation, religion or belief'; that the NHS 'aspires to the highest standards of excellence and professionalism'; and that it 'is committed to providing best value for taxpayers' money and the most effective, fair and sustainable use of finite resources' (NHS, 2010).

The mission statement and core values of the University of Cambridge are typical of the higher education sector:

> The mission of the University of Cambridge is to contribute to society through the pursuit of education, learning, and research at the highest international levels of excellence. The University's core values are as follows:
>
> - freedom of thought and expression
> - freedom from discrimination.
>
> (University of Cambridge, 2010)

Such statements reflect both the aspirations of an institution and the self-image that it wishes to promote. In any dialogue with an institution about values, principles or ethics, it will be helpful to refer explicitly to such statements. Often much of what a chaplain wants to say will not conflict with the values expressed there but rather reaffirm them and point out where activities or policies are in conflict with the institution's core values. Being careful to use the language of the institution in such conversations can be much more productive than choosing to use faith-specific terminology for similar values. Likewise, in any debate about competing goods or about the value of a particular activity it will be helpful, even necessary, especially where additional funding is being sought, to point out how the value or activity under consideration contributes to the institution's stated mission and values.

There may also be other values that are deeply embedded within the institution but that are not so readily made public. That is not to say that they are kept secret but they may not be readily voiced or even recognized. There could, for example, be deeply held cultural assumptions within an institution that may not be recognized as values but that can be profoundly important in institutional decision-making. Skills honed in biblical interpretation – in exercising a 'hermeneutic of suspicion' as to what interests are actually being served in official texts and policies rather than simply taking them at face value – can be valuable here! For example, there might be an unintentional yet ingrained class bias in the values and practices of a university. Other instances may be apparently neutral tacit assumptions, such as that confidentiality will always trump transparency and accountability or vice versa.

A further area to explore is what the actual drivers are behind decision-making within the organization. Thus while an institution may write about 'the pursuit of education, learning and research' or 'providing quality patient care', many day-to-day decisions may well be financially motivated. As noted above, this is not necessarily a bad thing in itself. The task of making strategic decisions and managing budgets is a complex one, and ensuring that money is spent wisely is important.

Discerning the values that drive decision-making is not an easy task. A good place to start is by looking through the institution's internal strategic plans or similar future-directed planning documents such as a five- or ten-year plan. These will sometimes be publicly available but more often will be internal documents. However, they may well be available on request, especially in the context of a job applicant asking for background information about the institution or, if necessary, via a Freedom of Information request. Such documents address the question of how exactly the institution is planning to go about fulfilling its mission statement in the immediate future, and can therefore show which parts of the statement are being given priority.

Identifying the chaplaincy role

In many large institutions the overarching mission statement of the institution will be supplemented by mission statements for each department within it, clarifying how that department will contribute to the overall mission. Chaplaincy may well be one such department, and it can be very helpful for an institution to have a clearly expressed sense of what chaplaincy is for and how it contributes to the life and work of the institution. For example, the statement of purpose for the Prison Service chaplaincy reads:

> The Chaplaincy is committed to serving the needs of prisoners, staff and religious traditions by engaging all human experience. We will work collaboratively, respecting the integrity of each tradition and discipline. We believe that faith and the search for meaning directs and inspires life, and are committed to providing sacred spaces and dedicated teams to deepen and enrich human experience. *We contribute to the care of prisoners to enable them to lead law-abiding and useful lives in custody and after release.*
>
> (HM Prison Service, 2004; emphasis added)

The italicized sentence exactly mirrors the language of the overall Prison Service statement of purpose quoted earlier and so firmly situates the chaplaincy role within the overall aims of the institution. This is helpful in a number of ways. It gives official approval to any activities that demonstrably contribute to the furthering of the stated aims, implies that the institution has already assessed and approved the value of chaplaincy and provides a mutually acceptable language and vocabulary that can be used to discuss chaplaincy within the institution. It also tacitly commits the institution to resourcing and training in pursuit of these aims.

Even where precise definitions of the scope of chaplaincy are lacking there may well exist reports, reviews or other internal documents that can be helpful in identifying both the values of the institution in relation to chaplaincy and how chaplaincy is seen as contributing to the ethos and service delivery of the institution. One obvious place to start is with job descriptions and even job advertisements. In the contemporary world it is very common for every job vacancy that comes up to have to be reviewed to see whether the post is still necessary or valuable to the institution. The shape of the post will often be redrawn to fit new perceived needs before being advertised. This means that job advertisements and descriptions will often reflect the most current thinking of the institution about the value and scope of the post in a way that may not yet be reflected in reports or mission statements, which tend to have a longer life cycle.

Obviously it can be problematic when there is a lack of any coherent rationale for chaplaincy. Reflecting on her time as a chaplain in a further-education college, Clare McBeath (Chapter 6) clearly identifies this as a key factor in making her job unmanageable. Since there was no clear sense of what chaplains were for, there was no realistic allocation of resources or of supporting structures.

Tensions

The chaplains in this volume identify a range of tensions that they experience in their work. Some are the result of value clashes or perceived value clashes, such as the tension between faith language and secularism discussed above. Others involve a more subtle mismatch of values, sometimes between chaplain and institution and sometimes between chaplain and church. Still others are more generic to all ministry, even all work, such as pressures on time and resources. These can be grouped into the following areas, which the rest of this chapter explores in more detail:

- apathy/hostility to religion
- a concern for equality of provision that obscures differences
- a focus on measurable results
- a lack of clarity about what chaplaincy brings that is distinctive
- issues of time, resourcing and support
- tensions with the Church.

Apathy/hostility to religion

Several of the contributors identify a deeply ingrained suspicion of or hostility to organized religion as a problematic part of the culture of the institutions in which they serve. This tends to emerge only as decisions are made and priorities debated.

It is worth noting two distinct subsets within this tension. In some settings it is experienced as an active hostility to religion. This can be a particular issue for university chaplains, where religious faith may be further perceived as compromising academic excellence by presupposing certain answers or precluding rigorous questioning. In other contexts the issue may be more that fear of causing offence can lead to a view that it would be safer to keep religion out of things altogether. Often one of the main issues is a lack of understanding about the requirements and sensitivities of different religious groups – a point made by Ian Maher (Chapter 8).

In either event it can be helpful for people of different faiths to join together in pointing out that ignoring their faiths does not mean that they are being treated equally with those of no faith but that the latter are in fact being given preferential treatment. If such a case can be made, along with constructive suggestions as to how faiths may be satisfactorily incorporated into a particular ceremony or facility, it has a good chance of success.

A concern for equality of provision that obscures differences

Even where the atmosphere is one of a vague sense of goodwill towards religion, the sense that provision has to be equal can be problematic since different religions have different needs in terms of provision. Examples of the sorts of issues that can arise in relation to spaces shared by different faiths are discussed in more detail by Andrew Todd in Chapter 23. Similar questions can arise in relation to the provision of chaplains themselves, especially where it is not economically viable or practical to recruit a chaplain from every major faith grouping.

This was the impetus behind a major 'faith review' carried out by Durham University that provides a case study for the way in which a secular institution may approach such issues. Chaplaincy had developed in the university in a fairly haphazard way over the 175 years of its existence. Provision inevitably varied considerably from college to college and faith to faith. Of particular concern to the university authorities was the fear that such variation in provision would be hard to justify in the external quality audits that every university, in common with many other organizations receiving public funds, has to undergo. On the one hand, if chaplaincy were perceived as relatively 'value-less' then it would be hard to justify spending money on it. On the other, if chaplains were regarded as a valuable resource then the university would face hard questions about the relatively poor provision of chaplaincy to members of some faiths and members of some colleges.

As a further complication and motivation for the review, financial pressures on universities meant that recruiting fee-paying students from overseas was increasingly important. There was a concern that the historically Christian nature of the university's chaplaincy provision might be a drawback in marketing the university in some countries, giving the erroneous impression that the university was a Christian institution.

The review process began by questioning whether a secular institution should fund 'faith support' at all. It concluded that it should, on four grounds: 'history, tradition and the university's foundation'; 'market position, recruitment, internationalization and diversity';'personal development and the role of spirituality'; and 'raising religious intelligence and the university's role in interfaith dialogue and promoting cultural understanding'. On the basis of these areas of legitimate concern to the university, the review concluded that: 'The University's provision of faith support should be re-affirmed and extended so as to reflect and encourage, in as equitable way as is possible, the diversity of faiths to be found among staff and students' (Durham University, 2009). This conclusion reflects an aspiration rather than a firm recommendation since it was clear from the beginning of the process that there were to be no additional funds available for the provision of additional chaplains from other faiths. Instead the hope was expressed that future vacancies would be filled in such a way as to broaden the representation of different faiths within the chaplaincy personnel. Although it was recognized that this might not happen in practice, the report was widely considered to have done its job since its very existence was proof of the university's commitment to equality and diversity.

A focus on measurable results

In common with many companies and organizations, the large institutions that employ chaplains increasingly demand measurable results by which to monitor the effectiveness of their systems and policies. This can be a particular source of stress for chaplains, as Ian Maher (Chapter 8) identifies. With the 2010 budget announcing 25 per cent cuts to public sector spending, the pressure to show evidence of effectiveness or value is likely only to increase. However, chaplaincy work is hard to measure or even inherently non-quantifiable; and all too often 'things that can't be measured – love, creativity, awe, religion, altruism – get forgotten by professionals and sometimes get ridiculed too' (Boyle, 2000).

Many chaplains see their work as essentially open-ended and process- rather than results-driven. How do you measure 'being with someone' or 'a quality of being there'? One response is to try to come up with ways of measuring precisely that. 'A ministry of presence' could be quantified at least in part by hours spent in the institution. 'Being with' people could be recorded in a time sheet or similar record of the time spent in particular pastoral interactions. Several contributors mention the importance of record-keeping for day-to-day handover and continuity of service. While this sort of accounting can be useful in providing evidence of demand or hours worked, one suspects that chaplains would view it as inadequate for expressing the value or benefit of chaplaincy.

Helpful in this regard would be the possibility of including an acknowledgement of the unquantifiable nature of much chaplaincy work in a chaplaincy mission statement or individual job descriptions. Nevertheless the pressure to provide evidence for the effectiveness of chaplaincy is a very real one. Unfortunately there is little evidence or research of any kind into either the effectiveness or suitable metrics of chaplaincy. Mowat (2008) concludes that 'the research literature as it currently stands does not directly or substantially address the issue of efficacy in health-care chaplaincy'. There are no obvious reasons why institutions and chaplains have not engaged with such research. Designing studies raises interesting questions about what might be measured and how. It would be fascinating to compare an institution where chaplaincy is well integrated – and well resourced – with one that is matched apart from the provision of chaplaincy. Differences in a range of indicators could then be recorded, such as staff turnover, client satisfaction, clinical outcome or academic results. In practice the complex interaction of almost infinite variables would make such a study impractical, but as a thought experiment it would be an interesting exercise, helping to identify where chaplaincy might be expected to make a distinctive difference.

The danger inherent in such an approach is of colluding with the view that only the measurable is valuable. Swinton has argued that while chaplaincy should be evidence-based, the nature of that evidence needs to be much wider than the limited metrics of a narrowly techno-scientific approach:

> Chaplains are first and foremost called to care for the spirituality of human beings, i.e., that dimension of humanness which refuses to be captured by standard scientific methods. If chaplains in their quest for 'professional credibility' forget this, they risk losing something which is fundamental to authentic chaplaincy.
>
> . . .
>
> Rather than becoming 'scientific' in the narrow, positivistic way that many other disciplines interpret and work out this word, chaplains need to reflect seriously on the possibility of expanding current understandings of science to include those dimensions of spirituality and humanness which are often hidden . . . (Swinton, 2002)

Swinton goes on to suggest that new categories of evidence need to be developed, arguing for the recognition of narrative as an empirical category. Accordingly, some recent research attempts to evidence the experience of those who have received chaplaincy care through hermeneutical-phenomenological analysis of their stories (such as Kelly, 2007).

On a personal level many chaplains will find that they are expected to identify objectives or targets in annual performance reviews or similar meetings. These are often expected to be 'SMART' (Specific, Measurable, Achievable, Realistic, Timed) and so bring issues of measurability into sharp focus. It is helpful to ensure that any such agreed objectives are in fact measurable, and vital to specify how they are to be measured. For example, if a goal is set that the chaplain will 'improve his or her awareness of multi-faith issues', the measure might be that he or she will attend a training course or satisfactorily complete an online training module. If the goal is that the chaplain will 'continue to deliver high quality pastoral care', how is that to be measured? By patient satisfaction surveys? By the assessment of their line manager? The temptation in completing lists of targets can be to make them as vague and thus as apparently unthreatening as possible – a dangerous game. If chaplaincy is to be taken seriously within a target-driven environment, it will often be better to insist on measurable goals, the achievement of which can be empirically demonstrated through qualitative if not quantitative feedback.

A lack of clarity about what chaplaincy brings that is distinctive

Arising out of the desire for specific, measurable results and often also out of the desire to demonstrate efficiency, several chaplains – such as Nigel Goodfellow in Chapter 14 and Clare McBeath in Chapter 6 – note that a lack of clarity about what chaplaincy adds to the institution can be problematic. The desirability of a chaplaincy mission statement spelling out how the chaplaincy contributes to the overall aims and objectives of the institution has already been discussed, but two further points are worth noting.

First, however important it is for chaplains to communicate in the language and values of the institution rather than faith-based jargon, it is vital that they do not get so 'institutionalized' as to lose their distinctiveness. What chaplains bring to the institution that it cannot get from social workers, mentors and so on is both an expertise in faith matters and an awareness of the spiritual dimension in life – to put it in secular terms – that arises from a deep grounding in one's own faith, as Mark Newitt discusses in more depth in Chapter 24. Maintaining the distinctiveness of chaplaincy while also communicating its value in secular terms is a delicate balancing act but a crucial one.

Second, a lack of clarity about what chaplaincy brings that is distinctive is not simply a top-down issue of the institution valuing chaplaincy. It can also cause problems in the day-to-day work of a chaplain if other staff do not fully understand the role and therefore do not know who to signpost or refer to them. For example, it may not always occur to a nurse to ask a distressed patient whether he or she would value the opportunity to speak with a chaplain, especially if the patient has not specifically mentioned religion. As Joan Ashton points out in Chapter 11, there is an important role for staff education here if those who would benefit from chaplaincy care are not to be missed.

Time, resourcing and support

These issues come up repeatedly as sources of tension, though they are by no means unique to chaplaincy. Chaplaincy, in common with much ministry, is often a role that will expand to fit the time available and that will never be 'done'. Much of the writing on clergy stress has focused on the blurred boundaries and role confusion that can occur in parish ministry (such as Irvine, 1997). While some of these might be avoided by chaplains, such as the need to live in tied housing that is considered a public space by others, many remain – especially for those chaplains in dual-role posts. The addition of the other tensions identified here can mean that chaplains are in a uniquely stressful place. Both because of this and because in many instances chaplains find their time being spent in distressing situations with those who are vulnerable, several of the contributors highlight the need for good support structures and supervision networks.

Tensions with the Church

Despite all the tensions and potential for clashes with institutional values discussed in this chapter, it is notable that for many of the contributors it is the wider Church that is identified as a major source of tension. In some cases this arises out of particular theological or liturgical differences. For example, Ruth Hake notes in Chapter 1 that chaplains in the armed forces often find that they are 'looked at askance' by members of their sending churches who feel that they are condoning or even encouraging morally dubious activity. Bill Burleigh in Chapter 13 identifies a specific point of tension with clergy outside the hospital context over language and imagery for the funerals of babies and children. As Mark Newitt again points out in his chapter, chaplains will often put considerable time and energy into identifying or crafting liturgies for their specific contexts. It can be a significant point of disappointment and stress when such work is criticized from a church point of view as not 'legal' or insufficiently religious, or when it is undermined by the language or actions of those not immersed in the situation. In the contemporary Church, 'pioneer ministers' in non-parochial contexts are often given specific permission to develop liturgies. This is something most chaplains do without feeling the need to seek permission, but for some it would ease tensions were chaplaincy contexts to be formally recognized as 'pioneer' contexts for such purposes.

Other tensions with the Church come from the perception, identified by several contributors, that chaplaincy is of lesser value than parish ministry. For example, in Chapter 11 Joan Ashton identifies with particular clarity that chaplaincies can be looked down on by some in the Church as requiring a skill level lower than parish posts. She is by no means alone in her experience of the institutional Church suggesting that someone who is not considered competent enough to be given a permanent parish post should apply for chaplaincy jobs. Yet as Mark Newitt describes and as the chaplains' stories demonstrate, the skills involved in chaplaincy are considerable. Chaplaincy roles can be uniquely demanding, and it is hard to imagine someone who genuinely cannot manage a parish post being successful in most chaplaincy job interviews.

Conclusion

These tensions with the Church force us to return, in conclusion, to the issues of marginality raised in the Introduction to this volume. Chaplaincy is, as the stories and theological reflections collected here attest, a challenging and rewarding vocation. Yet many chaplains report that once they take a chaplaincy job they find they are perceived to have marginalized themselves, placed themselves outside the boundaries of the parish system of the Church. Anecdotally one often hears about the Church refusing to select for ordination training those who make the mistake of openly acknowledging that they feel called to chaplaincy rather than parish work – 'Why should we pay to train you if we're not going to get any work out of you?' This is particularly frustrating to hear for chaplains who have worked hard to identify and foster a vocation, perhaps with a student or a member of the armed forces, who in turn may feel a call to chaplaincy work.

Furthermore, time spent working in chaplaincies is sometimes considered to be irrelevant experience when a priest is looking for a parish or diocesan post. Yet a chaplain may well have gained considerable experience of managing a team and/or a budget, and has probably received a great deal more management training than a priest who has spent his or her career entirely in parish ministry. Even more importantly, since chaplaincies so often involve working at the cutting edge of mission, they may well also have spent more time reflecting theologically on the nature of ministry and how it can best be served in different contexts. If the institutional churches discount or render invisible such skills simply because they have been acquired beyond their boundaries, they risk losing an immensely valuable resource.

Vocations to chaplaincy are not often routinely explored during ministerial training, mentoring or development. Yet such exploration can be key to discovering a vocation to chaplaincy, as Charles Thody's experience demonstrates (Chapter 15). Where chaplaincy is seen as marginal to the 'real' business of the Church, a move into it can be seen as a betrayal of vocation. Yet chaplains consistently report a strong sense of vocation to the jobs they are in and especially to the people they find themselves among. While some recent research has suggested that frustrations with the institutional Church may be a significant reason for clergy seeking chaplaincy posts, the same research confirms that many chaplains feel a positive call to chaplaincy and once in post feel affirmed by their (secular) employers (Hancocks et al., 2008). Although we asked the contributors to this volume to identify difficulties, tensions or sorrows they experienced in their role, these are far outweighed by the positives. In most cases chaplaincy is experienced in overwhelmingly positive terms as a deeply fulfilling form of ministry. As Jane Speck puts it in Chapter 10, chaplaincy incorporates 'all the aspects of ministry I thought I might need to choose between'.

Moreover as this book has sought to suggest, chaplaincy may be rapidly becoming a more normative form of ministry for the Church than traditional parochial models. Chaplains, as we said at the outset, are at the cutting edge of mission for the churches since they work with people where they are – in the workplace or in places in which they spend large parts of their lives – and so have access to a wide sector of society, including the dechurched or unchurched majority of the population. Churches should work hard to gather insights and experiences from chaplains since the issues chaplains face daily in their work are often, it seems to us, the very issues that the Church more widely will soon need to face. Chaplains appear to encounter trends in society in advance of the rest of the Church and so are a valuable source of information and experience about such trends and what religious resources have and have not been found useful in responding to them. Chaplains could perhaps be described as the 'research and development' department of the Church, and it is bad business to fail to invest in R & D in a recession.

In their many and varied encounters with people, the chaplains who have contributed here frequently report that they are valued not just as a generic pastoral resource but specifically for their religious functions or what they represent as chaplains. Offers of prayer and perhaps ritual, as well as attentive listening or practical help, are generally welcomed. Similarly the very presence of a chaplain may be welcomed as symbolic of the concern of God and/or the Church for the real lives and often the real suffering, danger or problems of the people concerned.

This is not a qualitatively different kind of ministry from the vision of a priest in every parish but it seems to us that it perhaps expresses that vision in ways that are increasingly more suited to contemporary society. We do not conclude that the churches should abandon the parishes for a programme of chaplaincies but we do believe that chaplains and chaplaincy provision should be much more closely integrated into the lives of the churches. Chaplaincy should be viewed as a normative and valuable part of the mission of the Church, as part of a mixed economy in which different modes of ministry are used strategically to reach different sections of the population that we exist to serve.

References

Boyle, D. (2000), *The Tyranny of Numbers*. London: HarperCollins.

Durham University (2009), *Faith Support Review Group Final Report* [Internal Document]. Durham: Durham University.

Hancocks, G., Sherbourne, J. and Swift, C. (2008), '"Are they refugees?" Why Church of England Clergy enter Healthcare Chaplaincy'. *Practical Theology*, 1/2, pp. 163–79.

HM Prison Service (2004), *Statement of Purpose*, available at [accessed September 2010].

Irvine, A. R. (1997), *Between Two Worlds: Understanding and Managing Clergy Stress*. London: Mowbray.

Kelly, E. (2007), *Marking Short Lives*. Oxford: Peter Lang.

Mowat, H. (2008), *The Potential for Efficacy of Healthcare Chaplaincy and Spiritual Care Provision in the NHS (UK)*. Aberdeen: Mowat Research.

NHS (2010), *The NHS Constitution*, available at <www.nhs.uk/choiceintheNHS/ Rightsandpledges/NHSConstitution/Documents/nhs-constitution-interactive-version-march-2010.pdf> [accessed September 2010].

Pattison, S. (2000), *A Critique of Pastoral Care*, 3rd edn. London: SCM Press.

Swinton, J. (2002), 'Rediscovering Mystery and Wonder: Toward a Narrative-Based Perspective on Chaplaincy'. *Journal of Health Care Chaplaincy* 13/1, pp. 223–36.

University of Cambridge (2010), *The University's Mission and Core Values*, available at <www.admin.cam.ac.uk/univ/mission.html> [accessed September 2010].